Globalization
and Social Exclusion

Globalization and Social Exclusion

A Transformationalist Perspective

Ronaldo Munck

Kumarian
Press, Inc.

Globalization and Social Exclusion: A Transformationalist Perspective
Published 2005 in the United States of America by Kumarian Press, Inc.,
1294 Blue Hills Avenue, Bloomfield, CT 06002 USA

The text of this book is set in 11/13 Times.

Production and design by Joan Weber Laflamme, jml ediset
Index by Robert Swanson
Proofread by Jody El-Assadi

Printed in the United States by Thomson-Shore, Inc. Text printed with veg-
etable oil-based ink.

∞The paper used in this publication meets the minimum requirements of the
   American National Standard for Information Sciences—Permanence of Paper for printed Library Materials, ANSI Z39.48–1984

Library of Congress Cataloging-in-Publication Data

Munck, Ronaldo.
   Globalization and social exclusion : a transformationalist perspective /
Ronaldo Munck.
      p. cm.
   Includes bibliographical references.
   ISBN 1–56549–192–0 (pbk. : alk. paper)—ISBN 1–56549–193–9 (cloth : alk.
paper)
   1. Marginality, Social. 2. Globalization—Social aspects. 3. Poverty.
I. Title.
HM1136.M86 2005
305.5'6—dc22
                                    2004015692

14 13 12 11 10 09 08 07 06 05 10 9 8 7 6 5 4 3 2 1 First Printing 2005

As we come marching, marching in the beauty of the day,
A million darkened kitchens, a thousand mill lofts gray,
Are touched with all the radiance that a sudden sun discloses,
For the people hear us singing: "Bread and roses! Bread and
*   roses!"*
As we come marching, marching, we battle too for men,
For they are women's children, and we mother them again.
Our lives shall not be sweated from birth until life closes;
Hearts starve as well as bodies; give us bread, but give us
*   roses!*
As we come marching, marching, unnumbered women dead
Go crying through our singing their ancient cry for bread.
Small art and love and beauty their drudging spirits knew.
Yes, it is bread we fight for—but we fight for roses, too!
As we come marching, marching, we bring the greater days.
The rising of the women means the rising of the race.
No more the drudge and idler—ten that toil where one
*   reposes,*
But a sharing of life's glories: Bread and roses! Bread and
*   roses!*

This poem, "Bread and Roses," written by James Oppenheim
and set to music by Caroline Kohlsaat,
was composed during the historic Lawrence, Massachusetts, strike
by women textile workers of many nationalities,
who in 1912 led the Wobblies (industrial workers of the world)
to a famous victory.
During the course of the strike
young women took to carrying placards with the slogan
"We want bread and roses too."

This book is dedicated to them.

Contents

Preface

Globalization is the big buzzword of our era, seemingly subsuming all other ways of understanding the world around us. It dominates economic policy making, social or welfare policies, and even the ways people contest the inequalities and oppressions that proliferate in the world around us. On the other hand, *social exclusion,* the other term in our title, is far less familiar beyond the corridors of Brussels where European Union "mainstream" social policy is debated, shaped, and implemented. My argument is that social exclusion—all the ways in which people are excluded from the necessities of life—is the necessary social counterpart to globalization. It provides us with a broad general framework by which to understand the social effects of globalization and, further, generates a common focus for those struggling against these effects at local, national, and global levels. The relationship between globalization and social exclusion should be set, I argue, within what I call a transformationalist perspective, which helps us transcend the divide between the "anti-globalizers" and those who believe the system can be reformed from within. Globalization both transforms the world around us and is itself changed by social, political, and cultural transformation. So, what does social transformation mean today and how might it help us in our investigation of globalization and social exclusion? According to the Oxford English Dictionary *transformation* entails a "dramatic change in form, or outward appearance," but it can also refer to a "complete change of form at metamorphosis." I take on board the latter meaning to capture the internal changes within society, not just the changes in outward appearance. In linguistics, on the other hand, *transformation* takes on a more specific meaning, namely, the process whereby a grammatical pattern or structure can be converted into another. Accepting that society is constructed discursively (how we name things), I also take on board this version to capture the struggles over meaning that occur constantly in relation to terms such as *globalization.* Finally, I borrow from adult and development education, where *transformation* refers to the way we

ix

look at the world dynamically but also, at the same time, at our own role in that world. A transformationalist approach is thus dynamic, complex, and reflexive. It questions what is usually taken for granted, including in "critical" interpretations, and it constantly interrogates itself.

David Held and his co-authors (Held et al. 1999) have advocated a distinct but possibly related "transformationalist thesis" to understand globalization as against the optimistic "globalizers" and the traditionalist "skeptics" for whom little has changed. They advocate a dynamic and open-ended conception of globalization. It is seen as a major historical shift, dramatically transforming the economy, politics, society, and culture, but in ways that are as yet not totally given. The future trajectory of globalization is thus open, and the complex global systems emerging are not consolidated. I believe that both *globalization* and *social exclusion* are terms that need to be deconstructed. We need to evaluate their underlying generative frameworks in order to transform them in the interests of social and political development. In an era of global transformations, such as the one in which we live, there is a unique historical chance to affect those processes by combating exclusionary and authoritarian tendencies with inclusionary and democratic strategies.

Roberto Mangabeira Unger (1998), for his part, advocates a species of "transformative politics" to overcome the debilitating opposition between reform and revolution. Rather than wait for optimum conditions for the latter, or "tilt at windmills," better to go for "radical reform," says Mangabeira Unger. When revolutionary change is closed as an option (as it is today for most observers/analysts/activists), it might seem that the only possibility is humanizing the seemingly inevitable advance of the system. If, instead, we take the transformative path, we can seek reforms that change the basic arrangements of society and politics, what Mangabeira Unger calls "its formative structure of institutions and enacted beliefs" (Mangabeira Unger 1998, 18–19). Society is changing rapidly as a result of the processes associated with globalization. The ways society is organized and politics is conducted are being transformed at a rapid pace. We need to rediscover our transformative vocations and challenge the dominant discourse that things are now "for the best in the best of all possible worlds," as Voltaire once put it, when patently they are not.

Karl Polanyi (1957) provides us with another transformative theme with his thesis of the "great transformation" of the nineteenth-century

Industrial Revolution that led to the emergence of the self-regulating market. This drive to "disembed" the market from any social or political context would come to fruition with what we might call the Globalization Revolution of the late twentieth century. But Polanyi also detected counter-tendencies to the drive by the market to rule supreme over society. What Polanyi called the "double movement" refers to how society inevitably seeks to protect itself from the market's drive to "commodify" (make it buyable and sellable) everything in sight. The very notion of a global self-regulating market is a utopia, and its social impact would be devastating. Thus, even from within the supporters of globalization we see calls for some degree of social and political control over the market. There is a drive to "re-embed" market mechanisms within society. Those affected by the deleterious effects of the market are bound to resist, according to Polanyi's theory of the double movement. Polanyi can thus provide us with a broad framework to understand the current "great transformation" being wrought by globalization as well as the countermovement it generates. Polanyi is a true theorist of counter-hegemony and the continuously reemerging human drive for positive social transformation.

Finally, the concept of transformation should not be conceived in a unitary or prescriptive manner. I agree with Hardt and Negri, who wrote that "Machiavellian freedom, Spinozist desire, and Marxian living labor are all concepts that contain real transformative power: the power to confront reality and go beyond the given conditions of existence" (Hardt and Negri 2000, 185). Other transformative epistemologies could be derived from feminisms and the alternative-development approach to build a broader, more pluralist transformative utopian project. This book is written in that spirit, seeking to contribute to a critical understanding of the rapidly transforming world around us.

Chapter 1 deals with globalization as both a threat and an opportunity for the cause of social transformation. It examines the various aspects or moments of globalization: economic internationalization, political transformation, and its social impact. The stress is on the complexity of these processes rather than on some beast of the apocalypse called Empire or Globalization. We deal also with the growing tendency to create mechanisms for global governance, despite the belief of some powerful rogue states that force suffices as a basis for international relations.

Chapter 2 turns to the second framing concept for this text, namely, social exclusion. Its origins as a European paradigm are traced, as well as the way it can become a new global lens through which to examine social inequalities and oppressions. Particular stress is laid on the global or international dimension of social exclusion, that area of social enquiry once organized by the term *imperialism*. We also review the various strategies or policies to promote social inclusion, that is to say, countering the old and new forms of poverty generated by globalization.

Chapter 3 examines the way in which increasing economic integration at the global level is not matched by social integration but rather by its opposite. The pattern of growing inequality reflects and deepens this process of social disintegration. We deal with the global South and the way structural adjustment programs and their successors have influenced society. The transition to capitalism in the former Soviet Union and Eastern Europe is also examined in terms of its impact on social exclusion. Finally, this chapter deals with the politics of inequality, that is, how global poverty is dealt with at the political level.

Chapter 4 continues with the themes of inequality and exclusion but with a strong spatial dimension. We examine the rise of the "global city," at once a symbol of globalization's dynamism and also of the poverty and inequality it generates. Poor neighborhoods in the North and poor countries in the South are both products of the way globalization generates sharp inequalities within and among nations. Finally, we consider the prospects for a global social policy going further than traditional anti-poverty programs to create welfare safety nets for those excluded from the gains of globalization.

Chapter 5 tackles the gender divide and how it affects and is affected by global inequality. It examines the differential impact of globalization on women, whereby some benefit from the new economy and others sink further into poverty. The so-called feminization of poverty is examined, as is the global sex trade, which turns women into commodities in keeping with the principles of free-market economics. Finally, we turn to the prospects of the variant forms of global feminism as a way to overcome women's oppression.

Chapter 6 turns to the ways race and migration affect and are affected by the various processes of globalization. We examine the "color of poverty," particularly in the United States, where race and social exclusion are so closely linked. People are on the move as a result of globalization, both at the elite level of the transnational capitalist class and as asylum seekers and refugees fleeing conflict and oppression. We consider whether, by analogy with South Africa before democracy, we can posit a system of global apartheid. Finally, we turn to the theories of a "new" form of citizenship more able to deal with migration and multi-culturalism.

Chapter 7 moves from gender and race divisions to those of social class. The polarizing dynamics of global capitalism today are examined in terms of the advanced capitalist countries and at the international level. Reflections on the crucial way the global and the local dynamics of class interact follow. Finally, we turn to the complex identities of contemporary social class formation and its political implications.

Chapter 8 concludes by looking at ways we can move beyond a world characterized by social exclusion within and among countries. Can the free-market economics that lies behind what we call globalization be countered by society and social mobilization? Do current moves toward some form of global governance mechanism represent merely a form of social control? What are the forms of contestation now emerging to challenge the discourse and practice of globalization? Finally, how can we move beyond social inclusion to a form of empowerment that could lead to genuine social transformation?

It is clear just from this rapid run through of the topics to be dealt with that I am working on a broad canvas. It is therefore impossible to do justice to all the themes, and interested readers must follow through with the references provided for each cluster of topics. This is very much a work in progress, seeking to provide a road map for the complex interactions between globalization and social exclusion rather than an exhaustive and definitive explanation of all their parameters. It is also a text that deals very much with the world as it is and does not deal with the various forms of contestation of the existing order. That it focuses on structures rather than agency is product of the topic and not the author's choice. My next book (Munck, forthcoming), currently nearing completion, deals precisely with the various forms of contestation that globalization has engendered that I take to be part of a broad, developing, Polanyi-type social counter-movement reacting against globalization and its discontents. The present text is written in a critical spirit that means it is skeptical of powerful institutions' arguments that we live in the best of all possible worlds, but it also questions some of the unthinking "radical" myths that are often just the un-thought-through opposite of the myths "from above." While "radical" modernist thought can break with existing conservative common sense, this is insufficient. As Sousa Santos argues, we need a "postmodern knowledge [that] will teach us how to build up a new, emancipatory, common sense. Postmodern knowledge fulfils itself only insofar as it becomes common sense" (Sousa Santos 1995, 48).

Abbreviations / Acronyms

CIS	Commonwealth of Independent States
CSGR	Centre for the Study of Globalisation and Regionalisation
ECLAC	Economic Commission for Latin America and the Caribbean
EU	European Union
FDI	Foreign direct investment
GATT	General Agreement on Tariffs and Trade
GDI	Gender-related development index
GDP	Gross domestic product
GNP	Gross national product
GEM	Gender empowerment measure
HDI	Human development index
ICEM	International Federation of Chemical, Energy, Mine and General Workers' Unions
ILO	International Labour Organization
IMF	International Monetary Fund
LDC	Least developed countries
MNC	Multinational corporation
NAFTA	North American Free Trade Association
NGO	Nongovernmental organization
NIC	Newly industrializing country
ODC	Overseas Development Council

OECD	Organisation for Economic Co-operation and Development
PPP	Purchasing-power parity
PRSP	Poverty reduction strategy paper
UNCTAD	United Nations Conference on Trade and Development
UNDP	United Nations Development Programme
UNESCO	United Nations Educational, Scientific, and Cultural Organization
UNHCF	United Nations High Commissioner for Refugees
UNICEF	United Nations Children's Fund
UNRISD	United Nations Research Institute for Social Development
WHO	World Health Organization
WTO	World Trade Organization

Globalization—
Threat or Opportunity?

For many people the term *globalization* has become shorthand for all that is wrong in the world today. Yet for others—the so-called globalizers—the changes it signals represent a unique opportunity for humanity to overcome hunger, poverty, and deprivation. Whether we view globalization as a threat or as an opportunity (or both at the same time) we need to address it (or rather, the processes to which it alludes) in a way that acknowledges complexity and avoids simplifications, if only because the issues at stake are so important. This chapter is thus designed to take the reader beyond the buzzword that globalization has become in practice. I address in turn various facets or moments of globalization from economic internationalization to political transformation, and from its social impact to the prospects for global governance today. In practice all these aspects are interrelated; as Scholte puts it: "While globality is a discrete concept, it is not a discrete condition. It is helpful, analytically to distinguish different spheres of social space; however, concretely, the global is not a domain unto itself" (Scholte 2002, 27). Bearing that proviso in mind I seek to "unpack" the various aspects of the globalization debate as an aid to presentation and clarity. On that basis we can move, it is to be hoped, toward a more holistic but also more complex understanding of globalization, considering its ambiguous effects and its still to be determined impact on humanity.

ECONOMIC INTERNATIONALIZATION

While the promoters of globalization in the 1990s sought to present this phenomenon of economic internationalization as something novel and breathtaking, the skeptics were quick to point out that it was not unprecedented. Hirst and Thompson argue that "in some respects, the current international economy is less open and integrated than the regime that prevailed from 1870 to 1914" (Hirst and Thompson 1999, 2). Indeed, in that classical gold-standard era there was a huge expansion of trade and a veritable revolution in transport and communications. Global markets emerged for many products, and the gold standard ensured a stable financial and payments order. However, this was largely a European "world" order, and the majority world was simply not included within its parameters. Furthermore, the disruption to trade caused by the First World War and the great capitalist crash of 1929 (and the depression of the 1930s) put paid to any illusion that a dynamic and stable world capitalist order could be achieved easily.

While it is indeed important to place the current phase of economic internationalization in historical context, we do need to recognize the massive socio-economic transformations that occurred in the second half of the twentieth century. The golden age of capitalism stretching from 1950 to around 1973 saw a remarkable flourishing of productivity and a gradual move toward a genuinely global free-trade order. The Bretton Woods international financial order, agreed to by the main powers after the Second World War, was premised on fixed exchange rates and closed capital accounts. This provided the legal underpinning for the multilateral trade order, and a long era of stability and legitimacy ensued. While this trading regime was clearly stratified and incorporation into it was uneven, it did set the basis for expanded capitalist reproduction across the globe. In a somewhat stylized manner I will now explore the various facets of economic internationalization in terms of the circuit of commodity capital (trade), the internationalizing or productive capital's circuit (the multinational corporations, for example) and, finally, the more recent expansion and internationalization of the circuit of money capitalism (finance).

From 1945 to 1985 global free trade predominated among the rich OECD (Organisation for Economic Co-operation and Development) countries. Following the debt crisis of the 1980s, most of the developing countries in the South followed suit and dismantled protectionist barriers. Then, in the 1990s, they were joined by the once-communist countries in the East that had to varying degrees been isolated from the capitalist market. A global market on this scale was simply unprecedented and signaled a massive expansion of capitalist relations and commodification (defined as the continuous generation of products for sale in the capitalist market for profit) across the globe. Based on data for sixty-eight countries, it was found that in 1950 the intensity of trade links was 64 percent (out of a possible 100 percent meaning all traded with all), but in 1990 trade intensity was measured at 95 percent (Held et al. 1999, 167). So, we can see that not only has trade been much more extensive than in the past, involving more countries and regions, but it is also much more intensive, as foreign trade became a more important component of most countries' economic activity.

With increased national enmeshment within a global trading order came a need to regulate and institutionalize that regime. The GATT (General Agreement on Tariffs and Trade) was a central element in creating a stable international trading regime following the Second World War, in spite of its weaknesses. With trade tariffs already reduced to a minimum by the 1990s, interest shifted for the more powerful nations to the question of domestic regulations governing competition. This led to the creation in 1995 of the WTO (World Trade Organization), charged with harmonizing competition and business rules across nations to promote global free trade in ever more sectors (to include, for example, services). The WTO is considerably more powerful than GATT was, and it has various sanctions it can apply. While the WTO failed to reach agreement on an agenda for future trade talks in Seattle in 1999, it has since moved forward, albeit conflictually at times, to ensure a rules-based intensification of trade liberalization for its 132 member states. The setback to the WTO's plans at the 2003 Cancún meeting does, however, highlight how difficult this process will be and how little genuine consensus there is for its strategy across the globe.

Along with the extension of trade went an enormous leap in production-level integration at a global level based on foreign direct investment (FDI) in particular. Perhaps the major characteristic of the postwar period was the rise of the MNCs (multinational corporations) that now account for the majority of the world's exports. Already in the 1970s a new international division of labor had emerged, with many developing countries achieving significant levels of industrialization. However, by the 1990s there was a much more marked global production (and distribution) system emerging based on the estimated 65,000 MNCs and their nearly 850,000 affiliates across the globe (World Commission on the Social Dimension of Globalization 2003, no. 159, p. 40). With foreign investment regulations a thing of the past, the main issue now was how to attract and retain

FDI, usually through national governments offering increasing concessions. The MNCs have shifted from their 1970s concern with natural resources and labor costs to an emphasis on efficiency and strategic asset seeking. As Dunning explains, "The strategic response of MNCs to the emerging global economy has been increasingly to integrate their sourcing, value-added and marketing activities, and to harness their resources and capabilities from throughout the world" (Dunning 2000, 48).

Globalization of production can be assessed in terms of increasing FDI flows and the growing importance of the MNCs in global production. It goes further, though, insofar as the global production networks are the key technological drivers of capitalist development. The impact of these worldwide networks of innovation, production, and distribution reaches deep into domestic economies, right down to the local level. It is estimated that the MNCs today account for nearly one-third of world output and approaching three-quarters of total world trade (UNCTAD 1995). While not wishing to minimize their importance or weight in the global economy, we need to recognize that the MNCs are not footloose, as many of their critics allege. In fact, the MNCs tend to be strongly embedded both nationally and socially, and in many ways seek stability rather than risk the uncertainties prevailing in unfettered financial markets, for example.

Apart from trade and production it is, of course, the development of a global financial market that best symbolizes the advent of globalization. Financial deregulation in the 1980s was accompanied by the growth of private international banks. The classical gold-standard era (1870–1914) had already seen the emergence of an international financial order, but this was largely confined to Europe. The post-1945 Bretton Woods era then saw a veritable reinvention of a global financial order. Consistent with national Keynesian economic policies, this financial order was designed not to interfere with domestic economic objectives such as full employment. However, this system collapsed following the US decision in 1971 to no longer allow the US dollar to be freely convertible into gold, thus undermining the system of fixed exchange rates. As Held and co-authors put it: "This ushered in an era of floating exchange rates, in which (in theory) the value of currencies is set by global market forces, that is, worldwide demand and supply of a particular currency" (Held et al. 1999, 202). Henceforth, foreign exchange markets would blossom and become a linchpin of the globalization strategy. With internationalization came deregulation of financial activities as the restrictions on capital accounts and exchange rates of the Bretton Woods order were cast aside in 1973 after an attempt to patch up the system.

Global financial flows increased dramatically in the 1990s in both their extension across the world and in their intensity. In the mid-1980s some US$200 million per day flowed across the globe; by the late 1990s that figure had risen to a staggering US$1.5 trillion. Deregulation of national financial markets and the removal of capital controls in the monetarist 1980s facilitated this move toward greater financial fluidity. Unlike the situation that prevailed during the early Bretton Woods era, it was now the international financial order that would take precedence over domestic economic policies. For many commentators, as Garrett puts it, "the potential for massive capital flight acts as the ultimate discipline in governments that may want to pursue autonomous economic policies" (Garrett 2000, 111). Finance capital is fluid and mobile, increasingly removed from any form of control despite the volatility and potential for disorder inherent in today's global financial order, dubbed "casino capitalism" by Susan Strange (Strange 1986).

The question we now need to ask is whether the combined impact of trade, production, and financial internationalization adds up to a qualitatively new era of capitalism we can call globalization. The globalizers who referred to a new "borderless world" (Ohmae 1990) and the "death of the nation state" (Ohmae 1995) were undoubtedly confusing tendencies (or wishes) with reality. We are now in the midst of massive economic transformations, the outcome of which is by no means certain. However, in spite of these provisos we need to consider very carefully the conclusion of David Held and his co-authors, based on meticulous empirical research, that "in nearly all domains contemporary patterns of globalization have not only quantitatively surpassed those of earlier epochs, but have also displayed unparalleled qualitative differences—that is in terms of how globalization is organised and reproduced" (Held et al. 1999, 425). Economic internationalization, in particular, has achieved a depth and extension that is simply unprecedented. Does this mean globalization is inevitable?

Certainly, there is nothing inevitable about economic internationalization and we need to avoid teleological interpretations that see it moving toward a predefined end, whether benign or the opposite. It is not an act of God or a natural event we have been describing but rather a process driven by social groups that are clearly defined. Globalization does not just "happen." It is a strategy for capitalist expansion on a global scale that began under the Thatcher (UK) and Reagan (US) regimes in the 1980s. As Polanyi wrote in relation to the first great transformation: "The market has been the outcome of a conscious and often violent intervention on the part of government which imposed the market organization on society for non-economic ends" (Polanyi 1957, 258). Global economic integration is today driven by powerful governments and corporations that think, design, and manage the new global order. These "managers" of globalization are now quite aware that free-market economics has very definite social and political limits and that it exacerbates risk, even for those who benefit from its unprecedented productivity. A degree of social regulation is thus increasingly seen as necessary if the free-market approach is not to end up in a state of social anarchy. This has been called the Polanyi problem after Karl Polanyi, who, writing toward the end of the Second World War, saw the growing gulf between the "unparalleled momentum to the mechanisms of markets" and the need for "society [to] protect itself against the perils inherent in a self-regulating market system" (Polanyi 1957, 76). As with Polanyi's fraught postwar era, we can truly say that this dilemma, or "double movement," as Polanyi calls it, is "the one comprehensive feature in the history of the age" (ibid.).

POLITICAL TRANSFORMATION

The economic transformations outlined above, of course, are also political processes and have massive political effects. As Held and co-authors put it: "Globalization today . . . raises an entirely novel set of political and normative dilemmas which have no real equivalents in previous epochs, namely how to combine a system of territorially rooted democratic governance with the transnational and global organization of social and economic life" (Held et al. 1999, 431). The main political debate today in this arena is centered on the role of the nation-state in the era of globalization. In the popular literature there was (as still is) a view that the nation-state has been severely weakened in its decision-making powers by economic internationalization. For the globalization skeptics this is an ideological position that seeks to "naturalize" globalization and absolve national governments from responsibility for economic matters. For my part, I shall seek to develop a transformationalist perspective on the contradictory political impact of economic internationalizations.

For many of the critics of globalization, from a conservative and from a radical perspective alike, "the traditional nation-state, the fruit of centuries of political, social and economic evolution, is under threat" (Horsman and Marshall 1995, ix). It is under threat because economic internationalization is seen to undermine national sovereignty and weaken the nation-state's economic decision-making power. In the new world order the very issue of national sovereignty is seen as a quaint anachronism (most clearly so after the war on Iraq in 2003). Economic linkages to the world market are seen as the key to security for any given population rather than old-fashioned notions of national security. As these economic relations of the global economy penetrate every corner of the globe, so the autonomy of the state declines. The market rules supreme, and political power can do nothing other than submit itself to its "laws." This new "borderless world" (Ohmae 1990) is seen by some to be heading back to the medieval period, before the Westphalian model of modern nation-states was created following the 1648 Peace of Westphalia, which brought to an end the Thirty Years' War. The neo-medieval (but also post-modern) global-village model now emerging, supposedly will be governed exclusively by supra-national political institutions.

In an era of intense global capital flows it is now argued by many that it makes no sense to talk about Italy or Kenya or even the United States as significant units of analysis. Nationalism, for the globalizers, is a refuge for losers only: "We don't hear much about feverish words of Hong Kong nationalism, but the people of Hong Kong seem to live rather well," says management theorist Kenichi Ohmae (1990, 13). By contrast, he argues, the nationalisms of the ex-USSR states or ex-Yugoslavia do not seem to put food on the table. So much for the globalizers, who may score polemical points but do not really analyze current events critically or in detail. But it is clear that the anti-globalizers also see the nation-state as irredeemably compromised by the forces of globalization. They call sometimes for a renewal of national capabilities but more often for local action against globalization as the way forward for social democratization. Both perspectives share a quite dramatic view of the decline (if not death) of the nation-state and its removal as a privileged arena for political intervention on behalf of transformation.

The globalization "skeptics" have, on the whole, contested this pessimistic view. Linda Weiss, in particular, makes a number of valuable points:

- economic internationalization (globalization) would not have materialized without the active designs of powerful nation-states and the consent of others;
- the globalizers tend to exaggerate the extent of the nation-state's power in the past so as to claim its weakening today;
- the globalizers "have not only over-stated the degree of state powerlessness. They have also over-generalised it" (Weiss 1998, 16).

Globalization has not simply created a brave new world in its image, as the convergence theorists have argued. Capitalism has distinct national variations, and nation-states have differential capacities to respond to the demands of global competitiveness. It does seem unlikely, on the face of it, that up until the 1970s the nation-state acted as a bulwark of national capitalism, and then in the late 1980s it suddenly became a mere "transmission belt" for global capitalism.

There are a number of theoretical weaknesses running through most of the positions arguing both for and against the nation-state's demise in the era of globalization. As Bob Jessop explains, there is a "false opposition [that] involves treating the state as a political force and globalization as an economic process with the corollary that their relationship is zero-sum in nature" (Jessop 2001, 7). This view ignores, on the one hand, the extent to which economic globalization is constituted through politics and, on the other hand, the continuing economic role of the state. The relationships among economics, society, and politics are much more interdependent and complex than this simplistic formulation allows. Nor can we conceive of the nation-state as territorially fixed in contrast to a totally mobile and "disembedded" capitalism. The reality is that the relationship between economics and politics is being transformed by globalization, and it is a process that cannot be reduced to a simplistic zero-sum game between the state and private capital, or between the national and international roles of governments.

We can certainly conclude that the nation-state has not disappeared in the era of globalization. But, on the other hand, we cannot continue to base our analysis of the world around us on the assumption of business as usual, as though nothing has changed. Two key theoretical interpretations of the contemporary state need to be considered now as a way of taking the analysis forward. In the first place, we have the notion of a "competition state" as developed by Phil Cerny and others. Free-market economics is changing the world around us and is placing economic competition in the role of core strategic value. This has transformed the status of the contemporary state, with its main task now being "the promotion of economic activities, whether at home or abroad, which make firms or sectors located within the territory of the state competitive in international markets" (Cerny 2000, 199). The state itself must become "marketized"—imbued with the values and priorities of the free market—to work effectively as a competition state in the era of globalization. It may not be national capitalist development that the state is now striving for, but it is still territorially fixed and bound to a particular population.

The concept of the competition state shows us how dramatically the nation-state's role has changed from the 1950s, when it was charged fundamentally with the economic task of promoting and deflecting a relatively self-contained national economy. In this complex national, regional, and transnational process of creating competitiveness, for Cerny, "the state becomes a critical agent, perhaps the most critical agent, in the process of globalization itself" (Cerny 2000, 205). The state plays a key role in the processes of "commodification"—whereby everything can be bought and sold including life itself—and deregulation on behalf of the economic liberalism that lies at the heart of contemporary globalization. It is ironic, of course, that the state is charged with driving back state intervention in the economic process. But this is not a state that is committing suicide; rather, it is one that is being reconfigured, re-tooled, and energized to deal with the challenges posed by economic internationalization.

Another crucial, and parallel, theoretical concept is that of the "network state" as a key distinctive feature of the present era. To deal with the challenges posed by economic internationalization the nation-state has had to become competitive, but it has also been reconfigured in the way it operates. The contemporary nation-state has forged regional and trans-national linkages as a way of dealing with the challenge to its sovereignty. The contemporary state also has to meet the social effects of globalization, with the increasing flow of peoples and intermingling of cultures (see next section) creating a much more diverse, and often conflictual, society than in the past. Regional, local, and nongovernmental organization levels of governance have become more important than in the past, and the nation-state has had to reconfigure substantially to accommodate these processes. Finally, the information era we live in is characterized by networks more than traditional bureaucratic organizational forms, and here too the state has had to become more flexible in order to deal with the new economic order.

These intertwined processes have led to what Carnoy and Castells call, quite appositely, a "new form of the state," namely, one where local, sub-regional, national, supra-national, transnational, and other forms of government are linked in a chain with "decision-making and representation [taking] place all along the chain, not necessarily in a hierarchical, pre-scripted order" (Carnoy and Castells 2001, 14). This network state has a certain "elective affinity" with the information era we live in as it is characterized very much—as with the Internet—by networks in which all nodes interact and old hierarchical forms of organization simply do not work. This is not to argue for a necessarily "progressive" view of the contemporary state. But we do need to recognize that the competition state also acts as a network state, something that has significant implications for decision-making and the way contestatory social movements may influence the decision-making process.

Finally, we need to add that we live in the era of the "contested state." The contemporary state is said to be at once too small and too big for the era of globalization. That is to say, it is too small or weak to maintain any degree of autonomy in terms of the national economy. But it is also too big or remote from the local level, where people feel alienated from national government. Thus the very status of the state is always in question, pulled one way and the other, lacking the stability and legitimacy the states of the advanced industrial societies had in the 1950s. At a global level the nation-state is also contested from above by transnational organizations, such as the WTO, acting as representatives of the global capitalist class (see Sklair 2001) that seeks to have the writ of "free" trade run unhindered. And the nation-state is contested from below by the counter-globalization movements that accuse it of selling out to the forces of globalization and of riding roughshod over the rights of the people. In the era of globalization the future is still open. We might do well to act on the basis that globalization opens as many doors as it closes in terms of the prospects for social transformation in the current era.

SOCIAL IMPACT

The economic and political transformations associated with the development of globalization are having huge social impacts. This section examines, in very broad outline, some of the main impacts globalization has on people. The degree of equality or inequality within and among nation-states is today the main issue at stake when the future prospects of globalization are discussed. As Göran Therborn puts it, "To the extent that it is actually operating, globalization puts on the agenda equality and inequality for the whole of humankind" (Therborn 2000, 34). For the advocates of globalization this is a process in which market mechanisms will not only create abundance for all but also will eventually even iron out socioeconomic inequalities. For its critics globalization is simply the most dynamic machine ever created to foster ever-growing levels of inequality. So the great riches generated by financial speculation, for example, are necessarily matched by vast layers of people falling through the very thin safety nets of welfare provision. Whatever our opinion, we must note the conclusion of the recent World Commission on the Social Dimension of Globalization: "It is thus widely accepted that the litmus test for the current process of globalization is whether it will significantly enhance the speeding up of development and the reduction of absolute poverty in the world" (World Commission on the Social Dimension of Globalization 2003, no. 172, 42).

According to the World Bank "24 developing countries that increased their integration into the world economy over two decades ending in the late 1990s achieved higher growth in incomes, longer life expectancy, and better schooling" (World Bank 2002, 1). Those that did not "integrate" into the global economy—such as the ex-USSR and sub-Saharan Africa—have suffered accordingly with poverty rising rapidly. While the World Bank does recognize that the type or form of integration is crucial to a beneficial social outcome, other organizations, such as the International Monetary Fund (IMF) and the WTO, put very few provisos on their optimistic message. Thus, more or less at random, we can take as representative the view of

Global Envision, a pro-globalization pressure group, which "takes the global free market as the starting point for reducing world poverty. Providing the poor with opportunities to improve their own lives is the catalyst for creating a more fair, hopeful, and stable future. We support economic development and responsible free markets as the most reliable and sustainable strategies for global poverty alleviation" (Global Envision website). This is not a view that allows for caveats or for the possibility that the road to globalization is not equally beneficial for all countries.

The optimistic view of globalization, however, can be countered with other data from official sources. The United Nations Development Programme (UNDP) found that at the turn of the century the assets of the two hundred richest people in the world were greater than the combined incomes of the poorest 40 percent of the world's population (UNDP 1999, 20). Another way of looking at global inequality is to note that the richest 5 percent of the world's population receive 83 percent of the world's income, whereas the world's poorest 10 percent receive only 1.4 percent of the world's total income. Such a staggering level of divergence between the winners and the losers in a process of economic development is surely unprecedented. Another way of describing increasing global inequality is in terms of the Gini coefficient (a rather basic measure where 0 represents equality and 1 inequality). According to World Bank data the Gini coefficient increased from .62 in 1988 to .66 in 1993. This may not sound like a dramatic increase, but it actually represents a faster increase in income inequality than that which occurred in the 1980s in the United States under the Reagan Administration and the UK under the Thatcher regime, when the neo-liberal offensive was at its height. The effect of globalization on inequality is a topic to which we will return in Chapter 2, but for now we must conclude that, overall, divergence prevails over convergence.

The second major social effect, after inequality, generated by globalization is interconnectedness. Ash Amin goes so far as to say that "perhaps the most distinctive aspect of contemporary globalization" is precisely the "interconnectedness, multiplexity and hybridization, of social life at every level" (Amin 1997, 129). From this perspective, territorial ideas of local, regional, national, and international levels are replaced by a relational theoretical framework. The world, in brief, is becoming much more interdependent in both a lateral sense, across space, and in a vertical sense, across levels of society and politics. We can no longer work with a notion that people live "in here" in their towns, villages, or cities while globalization happens "out there" in a separate "global" sphere. Rather, the global can only work through the local level or levels that make it up and make it effective. The multiple levels or scales of society are all linked through the various processes (economic, political, social, cultural) of globalization.

Life in today's big cities exemplifies the interconnectedness of local and global social relations and the complex multiplicity of scales that citizens structure their lives around. There is no longer a clear-cut and simple sense of community bounded by the space of a neighborhood or district alone. In a study entitled *Living the Global City* John Eade (1997) showed the diverse ways in which globalization had affected the residents who were of diverse social and ethnic backgrounds, had different lifestyles, and had distinctive perceptions and expectations. Rather than sharing as a community in a common local culture, the residents related to various global cultures with which they maintained a regular interaction. As Martin Albrow concludes, "People can reside in one place and have their meaningful social relations almost entirely outside it and across the globe" (Albrow 1997, 53). The locality is still a site for meaningful social activities of all sorts, but it can no longer be divorced from the "out there" (but also "in here") of globality.

The concept of hybridity captures well the complexity of social relations in the era of globalization. Identities are less likely to be fixed, authentic, and simple, as in the essentialist conception that once prevailed. Rather, identity becomes more fragmented and fluid, in a relational dialogue with others. We now have a multiplicity of identities based on nationality, age, gender, sexual orientation, type of work, place of residence, and so on. In short, our social relations are hybrids, no longer pure, and our identities may also be conceived of in that same way. We may well refuse binary oppositions—colonizer or colonized, male or female, urban or rural—and instead take up liminal positions, that is to say, "betwixt and between" fixed poles. The notion of border crossing captures well the increased spatial mobility of our era but also the greater social fluidity that characterizes it. From a hybridity perspective we can no longer neatly categorize people, as in the heyday of modernism, and it thus complicates our analysis of society and its contradictions.

The world is thus both more unequal and more interconnected that it was twenty years ago, but there is also more movement. Globalization, if it represents anything at all, would be the greatly accelerated movement of goods, capital, and people since around 1980. Transport has become cheaper and faster, oiling the wheels of trading. This has led some commentators to predict the "death of distance" as new forms of transport (such as air freight and containerization) facilitate international trade. The new information economy can practically avoid transport costs all together. We are moving from a world of structures and barriers to one based on networks and global flows. Whether it is information, money, goods, people, or hazards, we are now seeing global fluids that are escaping the lenses of traditional social-science concepts that were based firmly on the parameters of the bounded nation-state.

It is not only the movement of goods that has increased significantly through globalization, but also the movement of capital. Capital flows to the developing countries of the South increased from less than US$28 billion in the 1970s to around US$306 billion in 1997 (World Bank 2002, 42). Of course, this flow of capital was unevenly distributed, with the larger countries of Latin America, China, India, Malaysia, and Thailand receiving the lion's share. While the flow of FDI increased steadily throughout the 1990s, its impact on developing countries was still less than had been the case during the first wave of globalization. Thus, by the end of the 1990s, foreign capital represented 22 percent of total developing countries GDP (gross domestic product), nearly double the figure for the 1970s but still beneath the 32 percent reached in 1914 (Maddison 2001, 35). And FDI in the South is still only a quite small proportion of the global capital market, which is focused mainly in the North.

The movement of people from one country to another has also increased significantly since 1980. It is well to recall, though, that during the first wave of globalization (1870–1914) around 10 percent of the world's population moved permanently. Today it is estimated that around 120 million people (2 percent of the world's population) live in a country other than the one in which they were born (World Bank 2002, 44). A major impetus behind the movement of people is clearly the difference in wages between the economic North and the South. But if the causes of migration are largely economic, its effects are social, political, and cultural. For some observers, international migration is positive insofar as it may undermine national chauvinism and promote cultural diversity. But we must also bear in mind the somber conclusion of Castles and Miller: "Never before has international migration seemed so connected to conflict and disorder on a global scale" (Castles and Miller 1993, 260). This crucial theme is developed further in Chapter 6, but for now we signal that globalization has not just led to footloose and fancy-free capital but also to many hundreds of thousands of people on the move.

Finally, I believe there is a widespread image of the social dimension of globalization that we need to correct, namely, a conception of the global as dynamic and fluid as contrasted to local, which is seen as static and tradition bound. From this powerful image Manuel Castells derives the notion that capital and ordinary mortals live in different places and times: one exists in the space of flows and lives in the instant time of computerized networks, whereas the rest of us exist in the "space of places" and live by the clock time of everyday life (Castells 1996, 475). While this image certainly reflects a tendency in the social transformation unleashed by globalization, it may be too one-sided. For one, globalization is not something "out there," nebula hovering above the local. Rather, what we have been describing as globalization is constructed, legitimized, and reproduced in local and national places. Space and place are not separate in this sense. What this means is that globalization is confronted daily everywhere. Individuals, social movements, organizations, and social networks all have agency and are not powerless in front of a supposed globalization juggernaut. For every door that globalization has closed for social transformation—for example in reducing the scope of the nation-state—it has opened others, not least in terms of the vulnerability of the new global networked order to disruption through system instability as well as social contestation. What that leads us to is the topic of the next section: global governance, or how globalization is to be sustained.

GLOBAL GOVERNANCE

An obvious question we now need to ask is whether the socioeconomic and political transformations achieved by the complex process known as globalization are sustainable socially, politically, and ecologically. The Economic Commission for Latin America and the Caribbean (ECLAC) in a broad review of globalization and development today refers to a "disturbing problem," namely, "the absence of a suitable form of governance in the contemporary world, not only in economic terms (as has become particularly evident in the financial sector) but in many other areas as well" (ECLAC 2002, 1). Governance, much as the contemporary state, relies on networks much more than on the traditional institutions of government such as parliaments or congresses. It reflects the complexity of the global era insofar as it is a multiplex process operating at a range of levels or scales from the local through to the global. Since the late 1990s there has been mounting concern among the international economic institutions around the need to create the basis for good governance, which, I would argue, must also mean sustainable governance.

Globalization has greatly magnified the level of risk we all live under, insofar as the hazards posed by the processes of globalization are practically unlimited in time and space in the sense that we do know where this greatly accelerated world is heading. In the era of global risks there is an ever-present danger of a transnational financial meltdown, a global ecological disaster, and the ever-growing threat of global terrorism and counter-terrorism that has unleashed a new era of turbulence. What we can now add to this list is the so-called inequality risk, which is not of course unrelated to the threat of terrorism. Nancy Birdsall, at one time a senior manager at the World Bank, points to how globalization increases the risk of increasing income inequality in developing countries, but her concern is mainly over "the political risk in the short term of a backlash against the market reforms" (Birdsall 1999, 1). Birdsall enunciates a novel distinction between a constructive inequality that creates incentives and a destructive inequality based on denial of access to the assets that generate income. Even without accepting this divide between a "good" and a "bad" form of inequality, it is clear that it poses increased risks for all, whether those suffering from it or those who in power who may face the effects of a backlash.

The question of risk has always been a problem for capitalism. When Karl Polanyi was writing at the close of the Second World War, he saw the crucial problem as how unregulated markets could be reconciled with a degree of stability in social and economic life. This is essentially the same issue, albeit scaled up to the global level, that the governance problematic seeks to address today. Throughout the postwar period, up until around 1980, the system that prevailed can be called embedded liberalism (see Ruggie 1982), which alludes to the combination of international economic openness with varying degrees of social protection at the level of the nation-state. However, not only did the system of embedded liberalism never spread worldwide (for example, to the developing world), but it has been called into question since 1980 with the development and consolidation of what we call the era of globalization. So what other mechanisms can be used to ensure a resolution of the Polanyi problem today?

Contemporary global governance really became an issue in the 1990s, following the rise and decline of the so-called Washington Consensus, a set of global norms underpinning economic internationalization in the ascendant phase. Building on the austerity drives of the Reagan and Thatcher periods, this world view barely tolerated governance at all. Indeed, it was based equally on the absolute preeminence of market forces, the need to deregulate economic affairs, and the need to drive all forms of state intervention out of the market arena. For the developing countries, the recipe was one of dramatic structural adjustment, which essentially entailed a set of so-called market reforms (deregulation, privatization, and liberalization) to eliminate any state intervention or even attempts to regulate relations with the imperialist system. Governance during the heyday of the Washington Consensus was hardly associated with democracy (indeed, still seen as dangerous in some quarters) but more with efficiency and effectiveness defined in purely market terms.

The Washington Consensus was created by the US Treasury, but in close association with the IMF and the World Bank (which later was gradually to distance itself from the model). While this ideology clung to the neoclassical dictum that globalization would reduce social inequalities, in practice it could not deal with the emerging contradictions of the model. The newly deregulated financial and currency markets were proving extremely volatile, a point brought home forcefully by the late 1990s East Asian crises. Also, the powerful states that had promoted economic internationalization in the first place were finding that their domestic policy options were being dangerously narrowed. Jon Pierre and Guy Peters point to a third linkage between globalization and transnational governance "associated with the decreasing efficiency of traditional domestic instruments of control such as law and regulation" (Pierre and Peters 2000, 59). In essence, then, the structures of governance at the turn of the century would have to be adapted to the new social and economic realities of the era.

As Richard Higgott puts it: "Moves to flag up "governance issues" have been part of the attempt by the international financial institutions to dig themselves out of the intellectual corner into which their adherence to unfettered market ideals had forced them in the 1990s" (Higgott 2002, 20). Of course, it was not only the intellectual cul-de-sac that motivated the turn toward a post–Washington Consensus but also the real-world problems of political and economic instability and the no longer hideable increase in social inequality at a

global level. The buzzwords *deregulation* and *liberalization* on behalf of "free-market forces" were no longer credible. By the late
1990s and early 2000s the international economic institutions (led
by the World Bank) began to articulate new buzzwords, such as *governance* and *civil society*. It was now understood that the market
needed to the socially embedded and that some kind of safety net
needed to be provided for the losers in the great global competitiveness race.

As the post–Washington Consensus came to prevail, so the notion
of global governance became popularized but also to some extent
overgeneralized. As with the notion of global civil society (see Kaldor
2003) there is a conceptual vagueness and political "woolliness" that
hinders clear analysis. From the World Bank to the United Nations,
from the NGOs to the WTO, all agreed that the market had to be
regulated to some extent, but democracy, indeed politics as a whole,
took a clear back seat in terms of priorities. The various global summits of the late 1990s and early 2000s—on global warming, on
women, and so on—brought together a carefully choreographed set
of actors from civil society (in practice, the NGOs) to dialogue with
the powerful international economic organizations on a clearly unequal basis. In the long run the post–Washington Consensus is as
likely to be challenged as its predecessor was by the disparate social, political, cultural, and religious groupings left out in the cold
by globalization.

If the post–Washington Consensus was still based on a "top down"
conception of governance, a different and more "bottom up" contestation of the new global order also emerged from the seminal protests at Seattle against the WTO in 1999 and onward. The anti- or
counter-globalization movement articulated a disparate set of social
and cultural forces that significantly changed the tenor of the globalization discourse. This dominant discourse was now on the defensive and had to explain (or explain away) the rise in social inequality
and environmental degradation that it had unleashed. It also led to a
form of "new governance" that was much more attuned to bottom-
up perspectives, where civil society could actually articulate projects
autonomously in relation to the dominant economic order. From this
perspective, globalization in the twenty-first century will need to
negotiate a form of governance that has legitimacy among the population at large and is not just imposed unilaterally as occurred in the
heyday of neo-liberalism.

According to the new-governance theorists "any attempt on the part of government to impose its authority will be met with resistance and evasion, and . . . this evasion is likely to be successful" (Pierre and Peters 2000, 45). Even if it is not entirely successful in its own terms, it is most certainly changing the terms of the debates, most notably in reintroducing the principles of democracy and equality that had simply been brushed aside by neo-liberalism in the 1980s and 1990s as issues that were incompatible with competitiveness and efficiency. The movement for global democratization takes many forms and operates at many different levels or scales. It operates as a network that takes organizational form at times, but it is broader than these organizations. Global democratization or global justice movements are now an integral part of the globalization discursive domain, which promotes emancipatory knowledge, engages in cross-cultural dialogue, and also becomes involved in concrete reform measures such as the Tobin Tax (on international currency transactions) and various transitional measures to regulate globalization.

CONCLUSION

This chapter has reviewed the broad economic, political, and social parameters and effects of that complex ongoing phenomena known as globalization. Whatever view is taken in these sometimes fraught debates, at least the issues of development, poverty, and equity are now back on the international agenda. Returning now to our opening question of whether globalization represents a threat or an opportunity in relation to progressive social transformation, we must conclude that it represents both. Certainly there is no point in pretending that it can be business as usual for democratic social change via national states and their governments. The descent into barbarism that Karl Polanyi feared when he saw free markets becoming rampant as the Second World War closed is still a distinct possibility, especially since the attacks on the World Trade Center and the Pentagon in the United States in 2001 and the "war on terrorism" to which they led. However, the perceived need for international markets to be socially embedded and for a degree of stable political governance is greater than ever today. As Peter Evans puts it: "What is most important is that organizers of counter-hegemonic globalization have more on their side than luck and pluck. Elites, no less than the rest of us, need to solve the Polanyi problem" (Evans 2000, 239).

There is now a possibly unique opportunity to use the space created by global capitalism's dilemma—how to secure social stability and free markets at the same time—to democratize globalization and build sustainable structures and networks for good, that is to say democratic, governance. What I shall take as a working hypothesis to guide our enquiries on social exclusion in the era of globalization is the conclusion of economist Denis Goulet: "Out of the confrontation between the two globalization camps [pro and anti] there now emerges, however tentatively, an incipient mutual acknowledgment, still conflictual and heavily charged with suspicion on both sides. Each side, however, may see the necessity of coming to negotiate jointly the terms of 'another globalization'" (Goulet 2002, 37).

2

Social Exclusion—The New Poverty?

In the 1990s a new paradigm emerged in relation to the study of poverty in Europe. This was the notion of social exclusion that was arguably a broader and more dynamic concept than traditional notions of poverty. It is notable that Amartya Sen (2000), the international leader of poverty studies, has recently called for the adoption of "social exclusion" as a powerful new overarching concept for the study of human deprivation. Sen takes up the social-exclusion paradigm mainly because of its focus on the multidimensionality of deprivation and its emphasis on relational processes rather than the individual. This chapter traces the concept of social exclusion from its origins as a European policy paradigm to its adoption by international bodies such as the ILO. It then turns to the relationship between poverty and development in that part of the world dubbed the Third World, the South, or for the optimists, the developing world. We note, for example, that the concept of "marginality" deployed in Latin American debates on structural exclusion from the labor market in the 1970s actually prefigured current concerns with social exclusion. A third section deals with the specific exclusionary effects of globalization in relation to depressed or deprived regions (sub-Saharan Africa in particular) and social groups. Finally, we consider whether the notion of "social inclusion" is adequate to counter the social exclusion produced by globalization, and whether we need to develop a new transnational conception of citizenship. The purpose of this chapter is to "globalize" the concept of social exclusion as a new paradigm to explain the social effects of globalization.

EUROPEAN PARADIGM

The European Union (EU) launched its first five-year anti-poverty program in 1975 with a series of cross-national studies seeking to develop a common framework to combat poverty. By the time the third anti-poverty program was launched in 1990, the term *social exclusion* had come into vogue. The reason for this terminological shift seems to have been mainly political, namely, the problem some European governments had with what they saw as the accusatory, even radical, language of poverty. The concern of its third program thus moved from "poverty," loosely based on Peter Townshend's work (see Townshend 1979), to a concern with social integration of the "least privileged" in society. This conceptual reconfiguration helped launch the concept of social exclusion, which not only became a major driver of policy within the EU but was also gradually taken up as a powerful paradigm to describe the "new poverty" in the era of globalization.

From the mainstream EU debates on social exclusion emerged a definition that "refers to the dynamic process of being shut out, fully or partially, from any of the social, economic, political or cultural systems which determine the social integration of a person in society" (Walker and Walker 1997, 8). From this conception exclusion is seen as the opposite of integration based on a fairly conservative conception of individual rights. A government's concern with social exclusion would thus be driven by a desire to dampen any centrifugal social forces and any issue that might lead to a social crisis, whether teenage pregnancies or youth crime. Social exclusion is thus seen as a denial of the classic social-democratic notion of citizenship codified by T. H. Marshall (1950) around the civil, political, and social rights of the citizen. Although clearly preferable to the neo-liberal dissolution of all social ties in a market-dominated dystopia, this conception of social exclusion has at best a fairly diffuse reformist air about it.

There is also, however, a more active conception of social exclusion "defined as a multi-dimensional process, in which various forms of exclusion are combined: participation in decision making and political processes, access to employment and material resources, and integration into common cultural processes" (Madanipour et al. 1990, 22). Setting their concept of social exclusion within the context of contemporary urban politics, these authors provide a rather more radical perspective. The above processes—and exclusion from political decision-making is certainly crucial—are seen to be combined and taking their most acute spatial manifestations in the inner-city ghettoes and poor neighborhoods. Urban governance in the era of globalization is a highly contested process, and the poor are certainly excluded in many ways. What Madanipour and co-authors reintroduce centrally is the notion of power: social exclusion is not just a minor problem for social engineering in the era of late capitalism but a structural and inherent feature of an unequal system based on power differentials.

As the social-exclusion paradigm was developed and accepted by academics and policymakers alike, so its various formulations became more differentiated. The French conception, explicitly based on Durkheimian sociology and Catholicism, with its emphasis on moral integration, was at first dominant. Ruth Levitas has called this the "social-integrationist discourse" model; it focuses more or less exclusively on exclusion from paid work. From Emile Durkheim's conception of "anomie," the social-integrationist-discourse model takes its concern with the breakdown of the cultural and moral ties that bind society together, and, most important, the individual to society. Thus family instability becomes more central to this perspective than, say, the manner in which neo-liberal globalization has created mass unemployment and "flexibility" in the jobs that remain. In reality the social-integrationist-discourse perspective has been the dominant one in Europe including in Britain under New Labour since it came to office in 1997.

However in Britain there was also an older "redistributional discourse," which builds on the long-term critical social policy concern with poverty in that country. The redistributional-discourse model took its cue from Peter Townshend's definition: "Individuals, families and groups can be said to be in poverty when they lack the resources to obtain the types of diet, participate in the activities and have the living conditions and amenities which are customary, or at least are widely encouraged and approved, in the societies to which they belong" (Townshend 1979, 32). To be poor is to be excluded from ordinary living patterns as against the social-integrationist-discourse perspective, which saw exclusion in relation to an integrated individual defined normatively. Poverty is thus seen as a prime cause of social exclusion in this model, which also focuses on the processes generating social inequality. It could be said that this more social-democratic redistributive model took a step backward in the 1990s when it was recast in the new EU language of social exclusion.

Meanwhile, in the United States, a malign variant of social-exclusion discourse was being forged, namely, the "moral underclass discourse" following Ruth Levitas's (1998) useful typology. Taking the French concern with social order and moral integration to a new peak, this conception detected an underclass in society that supposedly suffered from a "culture of dependence" on the welfare state from which it would have to be weaned. This US New Right discourse of the 1990s emphasized the social behavior and moral values of the poor and ignored the social and economic structures that generated poverty. It is a gendered and racialized discourse that targets single mothers and young black men as particularly at fault. The moral agenda of the moral-underclass-discourse approach is explicitly rejected by the other variants but in particular by the still faintly social-democratic redistributional-discourse-model approach, which focuses on the structure of society as a whole rather than on the behavior of the poor. However, it must be recognized that during the heyday of neo-liberalism the underclass concept gained considerable popularity in Western government circles.

It would be wrong to conclude, however, that social exclusion is simply an integrationist concept and (in its US variants) yet another device for blaming the poor for poverty. In adopting the concept as an overarching framework for understanding the growing social inequality caused by globalization, the ILO points precisely to how the concept can be radicalized and globalized. But how can an apparently Eurocentric concept like social exclusion travel across the world, particularly to the South, where anything resembling a European welfare state has been very rare indeed? For Gerry Rodgers, who coordinated a major ILO research project on social exclusion in the early 1990s, the concept "has become a mainstream policy in the countries of the North, in Europe at least. In the South, its relevance remains to be established" (Rodgers 1995, 53). While it is easy to see how a Western European social-democratic social-policy perspective might seem irrelevant in the countries and regions of the South devastated by decades of structural adjustment and then neo-liberal globalization, the fact remains that globalization is having a similar social impact across the world and a common social response is called for.

It is also quite clear that if the opposite of social exclusion is integration, then the countries of the South have always been integrated within the structures of the world economy, whether through colonialism, neocolonialism, dependency, or the "new" dependency created by globalization. So it is not integration into a system but the nature of that integration that is at stake. Another clearly Eurocentric tendency is the blithe ignorance of the social-exclusion literature in relation to the Latin American debates of the 1970s on marginality (see Faria 1995). These debates were directed precisely at analyzing, for example, shanty-town dwellers on the fringes of the big cities who appeared to be marginal to the needs of developing capitalism. They did not even apparently fill the classical Marxist role of "reserve army of labor" played by the unemployed in the West. In both cases, whether it is countries or social groups it is the nature or form of integration that is crucial.

While the term *social exclusion* can certainly be put to conservative use, I believe it is now sufficiently detached from its European origins to serve as a global term for the social deprivation caused by globalization. There are three main reasons why global social exclusion can act as a broad unifying perspective on deprivation, unemployment, and inequality on a global scale:

- In the first place, economic internationalization has brought all parts of the globe under the sway of capitalist market relations. We need not accept rosy visions of "one world" to understand that globalization holds sway over the whole world. From a social perspective it is thus essential that we have a unified and coherent perspective to analyze its social impact.
- In the second place, I argue that it is quite outdated to have separate perspectives on social deprivation in the North and the South. While conventional development studies still works on the assumption that developing countries are quite distent from the advanced industrial societies, this view is questionable. The South and North are hardly watertight compartments. The South exists, in a way, in the great urban conurbations of the North where immigrants and many local workers live in third-world conditions. Likewise, the North finds its counterparts in the South in the high-rise buildings of the financial sectors and the gated communities where the rich and powerful live. This is another reason for one overall perspective on social development.
- Finally, it is clear that neo-liberal globalization operates with a similar set of free-market policies across the globe that tends to unify economic policies of national governments. A global social-exclusion perspective serves to draw attention to the social impact of neo-liberalism across the globe. It also allows us to emphasize the pressing need for social regulation of the market, which simply cannot be self-regulating without producing

disastrous instability. A global social-exclusion paradigm thus serves to emphasize that social regulation of the market is necessary if society is to be sustainable. It is very much in keeping with Polanyi's famous social countermovement to the self-regulating market.

In conclusion, then, social exclusion can serve as a powerful term to analyze (and combat) global inequality. It allows us to break with the economistic and individualistic parameters of traditional concepts of poverty. It is a paradigm that is multidimensional and multidisciplinary in the way it approaches social inequality. It is not static, as most conceptions of poverty tend to be, but is dynamic, focusing as it does on the ongoing processes of social exclusion. Finally, it is relational and understands that poverty has as its counterpart wealth and that globalization has generated huge levels of deprivation but also a massive concentration of wealth in a few hands. If "globalized," it can serve as a unifying analytical and policy tool to deal with the negative social impact of globalization.

POVERTY AND DEVELOPMENT

Traditionally, poverty has been associated with underdevelopment. While the West or the North may have seen an increase in poverty and unemployment during the neo-liberal offensive of the 1980s, extreme and extensive poverty had always been the lot of the Third World. Poverty can be defined in terms of not being able to acquire a minimum basket of goods to satisfy basic needs. Indigence, or extreme poverty, refers to a lack of the means of subsistence. Recently the World Bank has begun to operate with a somewhat arbitrary poverty line of US$1 per day; extreme poverty is often defined at around half of that rate. In a major end-of-century report the World Bank claimed to be returning to its central mission, namely, attacking poverty through a program of "empowerment, security and opportunity" designed to cut the number of these living on less than US$1 per day by half (World Bank 2000a). We need to ask why there has been a renewed interest in poverty and whether development is indeed the key to overcoming poverty.

Given that the World Bank is the most important transnational organization committed to the reduction of poverty, its conceptions and strategies have a huge influence, not least on the governments of the South. The Bank's 2000–2001 report developed a definition of poverty that claimed to go further than previous ones that were based purely on economic income. Borrowing from the work of Amartya Sen (1999) and listening to the voices of the poor through participatory exercises, the Bank produced a multidimensional definition of poverty that included income, education, health, vulnerability, and powerlessness. Hence the strategy of "empowerment" for the poor and "security" to reduce the risks the poor face in everyday life, not least from the vagaries of economic internationalization and the effect it has on developing economies. This was an important conceptual expansion of previous World Bank conceptions of poverty, but who was to combat it and how?

The fundamental tenet of the World Bank, shared by all proponents of globalization, is that "Global integration is already a powerful force for poverty reduction, but it could be even more effective" (World Bank 2002, 1) That is to say, economic growth, as *development* is conventionally defined, is the key to poverty reduction. We shall turn to that question shortly, but in the meantime we have to understand why poverty is back on the international policy agenda after having faded in the 1980s. The way the World Bank presents its poverty-reduction strategies is on the basis that there is general consensus that reducing poverty is a common good. In a major review explicitly addressing poverty in the era of globalization, the World Bank refers to a "fear [that] may not be universal, but does play a role in public perception [of globalization]," namely, that "it is exacerbating inequality, and perhaps even worsening the lot of the poor by eroding their incomes, increasing their vulnerability, and adding to their disempowerment" (World Bank 2000a, 1).

To address that very real fear, the World Bank seeks to invoke the powerful economic interests and the planners of globalization. It argues that diminishing inequalities can be good for economic growth. Taking millions out of poverty would produce consumers, and this is good for business. Increasing equity in the distribution of assets, such as land, can be positive for economic development. Reducing gender inequality can be presented also as unleashing the economic potential of women and this good for economic growth. The World Bank is thus speaking to the long-term interests of global capitalism and not the short-term, shortsighted calculations of the individual capitalist who may wish only to reduce wages and for whom social inequality is a great spur for entrepreneurship. What lies behind these economic calculations about equity and inequality is also the question of political risk to a system that is allowed to generate increased inequality, marginality, and exclusion on a huge scale without any control.

What the World Bank does not really address, in spite of its lucid world-managerial role on behalf of capitalism, is the relationship between poverty and redistribution. It seems an inescapable conclusion that any comprehensive poverty-reduction program would have to address the inequality between the poor and the non-poor. Redistribution of resources and power from the wealthy would certainly reduce poverty worldwide in a very significant way. Thus, the UNDP in outlining its project for "globalization with a human face" shows how the rich "could do a lot for world poverty"; for example, a yearly contribution of 1 percent of the wealth of the two hundred richest people could provide universal access to primary education for all (UNDP 1999, 3). If the assets of the three richest people in the world are more than the combined GNP of all the least developed countries, then redistribution seems a more logical poverty-alleviating strategy than seeking to "empower" the poor of these countries.

Being somewhat clearer now on why poverty has become an international issue for the globalizers, we still need to address the World Bank claim that "globalization generally reduces poverty because more integrated economies tend to grow faster and this growth is usually widely diffused" (World Bank 2002, 1). Economies that are more integrated into the world economy have indeed grown faster than those (such as economies in Africa) that have been marginalized. What is questionable, however, is whether the benefits of economic growth are indeed widely diffused. If we take Latin America as an example of a region that has sought to integrate with the world economy, we do not find support for that argument. After the "lost decade" (for development) of the 1980s, Latin America entered a period of vigorous economic growth averaging 6 percent per annum between 1990 and 1995; however, the number of poor and extremely poor (indigent) increased by 5 million and 1.5 million respectively during those five years. So, integration with the world economy may lead to economic growth, but the evidence is that it also increases inequality levels.

The belief that development and poverty reduction go hand in hand is one shared by many orthodox Marxists as well. Thus Bill Warren in the 1980s argued against the then-prevalent radical notion that capitalism would lead to stagnation (especially in the Third World). "Although introduced into the Third World externally, capitalism has struck deep roots here and developed its own increasingly vigorous internal dynamic" (Warren 1980, 9). For Warren, against the dependency theories then current, capitalism was the mainspring of historical progress, and its development was essential if a more humane society was ever to be constructed. This view follows, to a very large degree, the perspective of Marx himself, who saw capitalism as a dynamic and progressive economic force and capitalist colonialism as preferable to feudalism. Capitalism in the era of globalization is indeed sweeping away all obstacles to its development. Whether this will be progressive or not in the long term is still not clear.

Capitalist development is uneven, producing great wealth and great deprivation at the same time but, above all, the inequality that goes with unevenness. In its *Human Development Report* for 1999 the UNDP sums up the current dilemma in one of its subtitles: "Global Technological Breakthroughs Offer Great Potential for Human Advance and for Eradicating Poverty—But Not with Today's Agendas" (UNDP 1999, 6). The world is wealthier and more technologically advanced than ever before. Capitalist economic growth is entering a dynamic phase as it penetrates every corner of the globe. Yet new threats to human security are emerging, and social inequality among nations increases. Liberalization of trade may create dynamism, but privatization measures ensure its benefits are socially restricted. In terms of social development, liberalization is creating a huge gap between tradable and non-tradable sectors, and thus inexorably squeezing out the social and caring economy that has always been at the core of human development.

The 1970s debate on marginality in Latin America addressed precisely such issues in a direct way, prefiguring recent European concerns with social exclusion. The term *marginality* was coined to describe the situation of migrants to the city who were not even competing for jobs in the formal economy. The "marginal pole" of the underdeveloped economy was confined to unskilled, unstable, informal employment at best. Marginality had a Marxist usage expressed in terms of a critique of dependent development, but it was also taken up enthusiastically by the conservative modernization theories. In this latter form there was reference to a "marginal underclass" that could not be integrated into the development process largely due to the "culture of poverty," which created passivity and resignation among the poor. Brazilian development in the 1970s and 1980s in particular showed that the urban poor were not really marginal to capitalist needs and to what extent the vast sprawling informal sectors of the economy were an integral part of a rapidly (if unevenly) modernizing capitalist system.

Marginality, social exclusion, and globalization all come together in the term *Brazilianization,* coined, or at least popularized, by the German sociologist of risk Ulrich Beck. By Brazilianization Beck means to invoke an image of the spread of social relations and production patterns typical of the South to the imperialist heartlands of the North. Beck thus writes: "The social structure in the heartlands of the West is thus coming to resemble the patchwork quilt of the South, characterised by diversity, unclarity and insecurity in people's work and lives" (Beck 2000, 1). Neo-liberal globalization has created a great disruption of previously stable employment patterns, (re)introducing temporary, insecure, and "informal" employment in the North and even social marginality in the great cities. Brazilianization, over and beyond the slightly pejorative and Eurocentric ring it might have in Beck's usage, can be seen to reflect the globalization of the uneven development that once seemed to be confined to the Third World. On that basis we turn to examine in more detail the parameters of global social exclusion today.

GLOBAL EXCLUSION

My main argument in this section—and indeed in this book as a whole—is that the era of globalization requires a new conception of poverty and social exclusion. I start with the verdict of Amartya Sen: "The helpfulness of the social exclusion approach does not lie . . . in its conceptual newness, but in its practical influence in forcefully emphasizing—and focusing attention on—the role of relational features in deprivation" (Sen 2000, 81). The concept of social exclusion allows us to break definitively with the economistic and individualistic parameters of traditional conceptions and definitions of poverty. It does not focus on individuals but rather on the social relations that create and reproduce the complex processes of exclusion/ inclusion that lie at the core of contemporary capitalist society. It also explicitly names the causes of social inequality and focuses on the power structures of society not the global economy. It is not static, as poverty theories usually are, but rather presents a strong dynamic edge focused on the active processes of social exclusion.

To take the concept of social exclusion beyond its European origins it is necessary to "globalize" it. The developing countries have always been included within the global economy; the problem lies in the exploitative nature of that inclusion. So, social exclusion in the era of globalization must necessarily focus on the international relations of production, trade, migration, technology, and so on that structure the uneven development of capitalism on a global scale. This is a much broader conception of social exclusion than the one used in the EU as a social-policy tool. The international dimension of exclusionary processes is crucial for a proper understanding of how social inequality is generated and reproduced today. Perhaps paradoxically we also need to reintroduce the nation-state more squarely into these debates. As Charles Gore puts it, we need to "raise questions about the "nationality" of social exclusion, that is to say, the significance of the nation state in the institutionalization of exclusionary practices" (Gore 1995, 10). These points will frame our subsequent discussion of selected aspects of global social exclusion.

In its early European variant, social exclusion referred quite specifically to a type of society that was moving from Fordism to post-Fordism, taken as social models and not just a description of changing labor processes. Throughout the postwar period Fordism represented a stable mode of regulation based on mass production and consumption with high levels of social integration. As this model began to crumble in the second half of the 1970s due to the 1973 and later oil crises and the exhaustion of the Fordist work model, so the problem of exclusion came to the fore. Social exclusion thus can be seen as relative to a particular historical and geographical social norm, what is seen as normal in a given society at a particular point of time. For Lipietz and Saint-Alary, referring to Western Europe in particular, "To speak of exclusion as a process is a powerful tool to describe the phenomenon of transition from Fordism towards more precarious situations with a whole range of in between situations, such as long-term unemployment or part-time employment leading to the impossibility of reconstituting one's former way of life" (Lipietz and Saint-Alary 2000, 1). Instability, precariousness, and volatility are now general characteristics of the global era and do not refer only to employment relations.

What Fordism represented for the core countries, even in the peripheral Fordism of the industrializing world, was a certain degree of social integration. Employment, housing, lifestyle, expectations, and even leisure all had a certain stability and predictability about them. A stable link was forged with (and between) the world of work and that of consumption; there was stable welfare provision and even a (somewhat mythical) stable family life. All that would change in the 1980s and, in an accelerated fashion, in the 1990s as neo-liberal globalization took a grip on society. Now the watchword of the post-Fordist era became "labor flexibility" (Standing 1999), which translated into precarious forms of employment and insecurity of employment where once stability and security had been cherished. Along with the loss of a stable link to the world of work was loss of access to social, political, and cultural resources and the ability to sustain stable family life; ultimately, the various forms of the "new poverty" arose, which affected all societies subject to the neo-liberal offensive.

Social exclusion in the era of globalization also needs to focus on how nation-states are affected by exclusionary processes. There is now fairly widespread agreement that there are winners and losers in the global economy. The international drive toward competitiveness as an overarching goal inevitably increased international inequality levels among nation-states. For every nation-state that became a "tiger economy" (Southeast Asian examples stand out), there are many more that stagnated (such as the Latin American economies during the "lost decade" of the1980s). However, it is the countries of sub-Saharan Africa that seem most clearly condemned to a form of continental social exclusion as a direct result of the processes of globalization. Manuel Castells develops a striking image of a Fourth World, comprising veritable black holes characterized by the "exclusion of people and territories which, from the perspective of dominant interests in global, informational capitalism, shift to a position of structural irrelevance" (Castells 1998, 162). For sub-Saharan Africa this is a powerful if disturbing image.

Ten percent of the world's population lives in sub-Saharan Africa, but the region accounts for only 1 percent of global GDP. Most of the countries in the region have suffered deteriorating and volatile terms of trade for their exports. The region provides most of the entries on the list of least developed countries (LDC), as the poorest of the poor countries are known. We find that the LDC share of world trade declined by half between 1980 and 1997 as a direct result of the pressures of globalization. According to the World Bank the problem for the LDCs "is not that they are being impoverished by globalization, but that they are in danger of being largely excluded from it" (World Bank 2002, 2). Exclusion does in fact lead to impoverishment for the peoples of sub-Saharan Africa. Clearly, in this case alone we can see how the unfolding dynamic of globalization has simultaneously produced a growing economic integration among the different regions of the world, and a process of social disintegration for those regions that are not favorably integrated into the new order.

Where the national and the global become most clearly fused is in relation to the so-called global city. These urban conglomerates are defined by Saskia Sassen as "strategic sites" in the global economy with "high levels of internationalization in their economy and in their broader social structure" (Sassen 1999, 154). Cities like New York, Tokyo, London, Paris, and Frankfurt, but also perhaps São Paulo, Sydney, and New Delhi, are key nodes in the networks created by the new global economy. These huge cities concentrate within their boundaries a disproportionate amount of wealth based on the dynamism of the new economy. These cities orient toward the world economy and (metaphorically) turn their backs on the domestic economy. What they are creating is a new hierarchy among cities with winners and losers locked into a total zero-sum game. Competitiveness among national economies, generated by globalization, also translates into a race among cities to attract inward investment and to "sell" the city as an attractive locale for the global investor.

What happens at the local level within the global city is a huge increase in social inequality as it literally reflects the growing divide between the North and the South in the global economy. Alongside the high-income gentrified housing are the homeless, and along with the high-earning finance and e-commerce sectors lie the vastly increased informal sectors of employment. The increased presence of migrant workers from poorer countries serves to make visible how the Third World has become an integral part of the First, particularly in its large cities. These processes of social and spatial inequality and segregation follow an earlier trend toward labor flexibility under the neo-liberal governments of the 1980s designed to better secure capital's control over its work force. Whereas in an earlier period of capitalist development the city as a site of consumption led to some degree of social convergence, in today's era of globalization the gap between the rich and poor is growing steadily in the large cities at all levels from the world of work to housing, from health to consumption.

One thing that is clear from the above analysis of post-Fordist social exclusion, the social exclusion of nation-states, and the inclusion/exclusion processes inherent in the global city phenomena is that the relationship between globalization and social exclusion is a complex one. Certainly social exclusion operates at a local-community level, on a nation-state scale (the "nationality" of social exclusion), and on an international scale. These processes are always combined and cannot really be conceived of as separate, watertight compartments. Where the overall focus on globalization may be prioritized, however, is in terms of a unifier or common denominator of diverse struggles for democracy and autonomy against inequality, racism and sexism, and national/religious oppression. It is that struggle for equality in the era of globalization to which the next section turns.

The issue of equality/inequality within the complex processes of globalization is, indeed, the new social question of our era. The question to be addressed is whether the problematic of social exclusion can be used to challenge the various facets of inequality present in the world today. John Gray points out that, while the notion of inclusion is quite distinct from that of equality, we should be quite clear that "global laissez-faire is no less inimical to the project of an inclusive society" (Gray 2000, 33) than it is to that of an equal one. That is probably the case, but we should not neglect the discursive power of the concept of social inclusion as, after all, very few policymakers would actually argue *for* social exclusion. As we saw in Chapter 1, the heyday of Gray's global laissez-faire society is perhaps now over, and even in the corridors of power there is a recognition that stable global governance requires some attention to the social exclusion caused or aggravated by the processes of globalization.

SOCIAL INCLUSION?

The linguistic opposite of social exclusion is, of course, social inclusion, so is this the obvious remedy for the situation? The theory of social inclusion rests on the assumption that individual well-being is the key to social prosperity and development. Not only is this a very individualist perspective, but it also tends to "blame the victim" in the sense that the onus is on the individual to remedy the situation. It can also take on a racist dynamic as in the case where national governments argue for the need of migrant groups to integrate with the host society. This policy discourse in Europe, for example, is at odds with the more benign social-democratic inflexion of social-inclusion promotion. Above all, the notion of social inclusion tends to operate with a normative concept of the "well-integrated" individual who will have a stable job, good education, and strong family and community relationships. This individual is deemed to have the social assets required to achieve strong social and economic integration.

It is easy to see how the language of social inclusion, integration, and cohesion can take a conservative and, in actual effects, exclusionary dynamic, not least in its ignorance of difference. However, it is necessary to note that social inclusion can take on a quite different complexion. For example, the UNDP has advanced a global social policy program based on a genuinely emancipatory conception of social inclusion. For the UNDP, human development requires ethics (respect for human rights), development (reduction of poverty), equity (reducing international disparities), human security (reducing vulnerability), and inclusion (reducing the marginalization of people and countries) (UNDP 1999, 5). When we break with an organicist conception of social inclusion we are returning to the relational view of social exclusion. That is to say, it is not merely that individuals or even social groups exclude others from social goods; social exclusion is, rather, based on structural processes within society that systematically create inequalities and barriers for social advancement by the poor, the disempowered, and the oppressed in society.

Having introduced the negative and positive connotations of social inclusion as a counter to social exclusion, we need to explore the various practical strategies being advanced. The importance of the issue for global planners is not in doubt. Thus World Bank president, James Wolfensohn, declared in 1997 that "our goal must be to reduce these disparities across and within countries, to bring more people into the economic mainstream, to promote equitable access to the benefits of development regardless of nationality, race, or gender. This . . . the Challenge of Inclusion . . . is the key development challenge of our time" (Wolfensohn 1997). While believing that globalization is ultimately good for equitable development and human progress, the Bank clearly recognizes the risks it poses for the poor. It has thus turned in a more "social" direction, actively supporting NGOs and community social funds in many countries. Its objective has been to help the poor better manage the risks to their households and communities posed by the uncertainties and inequities of globalization.

In its ambitious Attacking Poverty Program of 2000, the World Bank argues that the core policies should hinge around "actions to stimulate overall growth, make markets work for poor people, and build their assets" (World Bank 2002, 8). What this means, in practice, is simply encouraging private investment and expanding into international markets. Building assets is seen to occur mainly through education, and then security can be enhanced through micro-insurance programs for the poor to complement existing micro-credit programs. Gender equity in particular is seen to be efficient in market terms as well as socially desirable. While recognizing that poverty is multidimensional and that poverty reduction strategies will be equally so, the World Bank conclusion is simple: "The poor are the main actors in the fight against poverty" (World Bank 2000a, 12). We are thus back with a "blaming the victims" approach that fails to recognize the structural causes of global poverty or to address the glaring levels of social inequality that have been generated, or at least exacerbated, by globalization.

A widely promoted strategy to develop empowerment among the poor has centered on the notion of social capital. When the World Bank began to promote this concept actively as the key to social development in the South, many analysts welcomed it as a departure from the previously dominant economism. The term derives from *civil society*, where a variety of civic associations knit together the fabric of society. These networks of trust and reciprocity—a sense of community essentially—are dubbed social capital in a direct analogy with monetary capital. It is seen as a resource. As Putnam puts it, "Stocks of social capital, such as trust, norms, and networks, tend to be self-reinforcing and cumulative" (Putnam 1993, 177). To combat social exclusion, then, social capital needs to be built in poor communities. While there are vicious circles of exploitation and distrust, Putnam points to the happy situation where "virtuous circles result in social equilibria with high levels of cooperation, trust, reciprocity, civic engagement, and collective well-being" (Putnam 1993, 177).

The concept of social capital appeared an attractive way to contest economism and to move beyond neo-liberalism. It also made visible the informal economy and the unpaid labor often carried out by women. However, while it is easy to understand how these informal networks of trust or cooperation may be a coping strategy for the poor, it is not readily apparent how they might operate as a poverty-reduction mechanism. Nor does a good stock of social capital (a strong sense of community, for example) automatically overcome the structural inequalities inherent in the world market or, for example, in gender relations. An even more fundamental problem from a gender perspective, as Maxine Molyneux argues, "arises from the conservative bias associated with most social capital approaches" (Molyneux 2002, 182), which entails building on "traditional" networks and, in essence, consolidating the "traditional" family. So, although the concept of social capital may well point us toward other useful areas such as community and civil society, it is itself part of the conservative communitarian perspective on social exclusion.

At a broader level, the struggle against social exclusion is being waged through the incipient development of a global social policy (see Chapter 4). Put most clearly by Bob Deacon, "Neo-liberal globalization is presenting a challenge to welfare provisioning in the industrialized countries and to the prospects for equitable social development in developing and transition economies" (Deacon 2000, v). While the WTO pushes inexorably for a complete freeing of market forces—to enter the health, education, and social-insurance areas, for example—other international organizations such as the World Bank recognize the need for some kind of safety net if globalization is not to generate too much misery and possibly opposition. Even the IMF is now beginning to recognize that some degree of social equity might even be beneficial to economic growth. Whatever the outcomes of these ongoing debates and political struggles it seems clear that there is now a domain of global social policy over and above the traditional nation-state level at which welfare provisions were developed and fought over.

While the domain of global social policy will undoubtedly be a terrain of contestation, it has certain limitations from a transformationalist perspective. It is, first of all, a top-down perspective that tends to ignores the importance and impact of the contestation of globalization from "below." Furthermore, as Nicola Yeates argues, this approach focuses on the supra-national organizations such as the IMF and World Bank and reflects "the institutionalist tendencies within academic social policy itself which privileges state institutions" (Yeates 2001, 130). The broader problematic of global governance (see Prakash and Hart 1999) is actually more attuned to the conflictual way in which globalization responds to contestation and not just rational planning. And, it must be said that the global social policy perspective is marked very strongly by its European (particularly British) welfare states origins. The issue of welfare and poverty alleviation in the South simply cannot be conceptualized from an optic that assumes an orderly social-democratic generation of a welfare state under Keynesian economic management conditions.

Finally, we may consider whether the emerging conception of global citizenship may be a means to deal effectively with social exclusion. The challenge is to construct a new conception of citizenship more adequate to the globalized times we live in than traditional nation-state based notions. With the world around us increasingly more internationalized in terms of the economic, political, social, and cultural relationships we engage in, so it becomes less possible to sustain a purely national conception of citizenship. Traditionally, citizenship has been considered from the point of view of political and social rights, conceived in a fairly abstract and universal manner. As Ruth Lister argues, the key political question today is how to generate "the incorporation of diversity and difference into the conceptualization of citizenship rights" (Lister 2000, 85) in ways that would accommodate difference without sacrificing the principle of equal rights. Full citizenship rights—in a multidimensional and active sense—are arguably the only way to overcome the processes of social exclusion generated by globalization.

CONCLUSION

This chapter examined the development of a new conceptual paradigm to understand and deal with all aspects of poverty, inequality, and oppression in the era of globalization. We related the new perspective of social exclusion to earlier development debates and more traditional conceptions of poverty. Put at its simplest, poverty in the era of modernity is related to exploitation, but, as Negri puts it, "In the postmodern era the poor are excluded and that exclusion occurs 'within' the production of the world" (Negri 2003, 198). The shift from exploitation to exclusion was thus a major feature of the emergence of a new globalized society in the 1990s and represented a distinct model of social development. On balance, then, once it has been "internationalized," the term provided many analytical insights that shall be developed in the chapters that follow in relation to specific social groups and regions of the world.

There are two major problems associated with the turn toward a post-modern social order that we will seek to analyze and overcome in the chapters to come. In the first place, there is the problem posed for social transformation by the growing diversification of social struggles. Hilary Silver notes correctly that "because of the new poverty's individualized quality, many of the excluded are isolated from one another, hindering mobilization or representation" (Silver 1996, 137). When social class was the mobilizing factor this served to unify the work place, the neighborhood, and families in a common effort. The new poverty of post-Fordism and the social exclusion logic now prevailing tend rather to fragment the various constituencies in social and spatial terms. The second main factor conspiring against a common global-citizenship platform is the overarching divide in the world between poor and rich countries, the developed and the underdeveloped, or in current idiom, the globalizers and the globalized. The language of rights—in an abstract and universal sense—has little purchase in those situations where the very conditions for human existence are precarious and subject to wars of aggression and civil wars. It remains for us to demonstrate that the social exclusion paradigm can provide a more fruitful transformative path through social inclusion policies and practices.

3

Global Integration /
Social Disintegration

It is an apparent paradox of globalization that the increasing global economic integration that it creates leads more to social disintegration rather than to social integration. Economic organizations become more "disembedded" from social relations and the welfare safety nets that once prevented social disintegration become less effective or token only. This is similar to the process Polanyi described for the Industrial Revolution that led to "an avalanche of social dislocation. . . . This catastrophe was the accompaniment of a vast movement of economic improvement" (Polanyi 1957, 40). The globalization revolution of our era was preceded by a process of structural adjustment in the South, the means through which this part of the globe was integrated by the globalization machine. This chapter traces the main patterns of inequality at a global level to test the propositions for and against globalization and then moves on to the transition from socialism to capitalism in the East, where particularly acute forms of social and economic inequality have been generated. Finally, we turn to the politics of inequality or, to put it another way, what is to be done in relation to the social disintegration that seems to be an integral part of global economic integration. If global economic integration is leading to social disintegration, what future does it have?

PATTERNS OF INEQUALITY

Globalization can be said to have placed the question of inequality back onto the political agenda whether we are arguing for or against globalization. The issue is crucial because, as Robert Wade puts it, "if world income distribution became more equal in the final

41

quarter of the last century, this would be powerful evidence that globalization works to the benefit of all" (Wade 2001, 2). While during the heyday of neo-liberalism the very notion of inequality had become invisible, by the mid-1990s, when globalization was in full flow, the proponents of the globalized version were themselves bringing it to the fore. Even the critics of neo-liberalism were beginning to argue that perhaps globalization at least had the potential to overcome poverty and underdevelopment, even if it generated more inequality. More rich people might be the necessary counterpart to fewer poor people. Thus Keith Griffin, a longstanding critic of orthodox capitalist development strategies could argue that "in recent years the pattern of global growth, contrary to a widely held belief, has helped to reduce inequality in the distribution of world income. For once, the proportionate gains of the poor exceed those of the rich" (Griffin 1995, 364). Rather than dismiss this optimistic reading as simply the propaganda of the globalizers, we should examine the objective basis for this argument.

The world has indeed changed dramatically over the last thirty-five years. Infant mortality rates have been reduced by 50 percent in that period, and life expectancy has risen by ten years (see UNDP 1999). The capitalist revolution that globalization represents has had incalculable social effects, and we cannot assume that all of these have been negative. In India and China millions of people have been taken out of absolute poverty. According to the World Bank, from 1980 to 2000 the number worldwide of those living in absolute poverty has declined by 200 million or from 29 percent to 23 percent of the world's population (World Bank 2004). From these bare statistics it is a short step to one-time Marxist commentator Charles Leadbetter's verdict that "globalization is an essential component of a poverty reduction strategy in the developing world" (Leadbetter 2002, 316). The problem is not seen as globalization per se but, rather, the failure of globalization to spread fast enough and extend its dynamism to all parts of the globe and to all sections of society.

In terms of theoretical explanations it is not only the neo-liberal architects of globalization that argue for its overall beneficial effects. In 1980, as globalization was only beginning to take shape as a global capitalist strategy, Bill Warren (1980) had developed an influential Marxist modernization perspective. Capitalism was seen as progressive in the sense of sweeping away previous modes of production and developing the forces of production. For Warren, capitalism was the mainspring of historical progress, and its development was essential if a more humane society was ever to be constructed. Notions of imperialism and dependency were simply forms of a nationalist mythology that was against "foreign" capitalism and not capitalism per se. "Although introduced into the Third World externally, capitalism has struck deep roots here and developed its own increasingly vigorous internal dynamic" (Warren 1980, 9). Even if we were to accept fully this dynamic and progressive vision of capitalism's worldwide expansion, which led to what we now call globalization, it does not alter the inherently uneven nature of capitalist development. From its origins until today the accumulation of great wealth coexists with terrible and widespread poverty. Furthermore, the development of some parts of the globe has its necessary counterpart in the underdevelopment of others.

The optimistic reading of globalization is also flawed in terms of its factual basis. The oft quoted reduction of the numbers living in absolute poverty was contradicted by the World Bank itself in its landmark 2000 *World Development Report: Attacking Poverty,* which concluded that the number of people living on less than US$1 a day had actually increased by twenty million between 1987 and 1988 (World Bank 2001a). It was only after Joe Stiglitz and Ravi Kanbur (chief economist and director of the *World Development Report* respectively) left the World Bank that other economists, principally David Dollar, found the figures to argue that the numbers living in absolute poverty had declined by 200 million between 1980 and 1998 (see World Bank 2002). There is conclusive evidence that the figures were manipulated (see Wade 2004 for details), and certainly we cannot place decisive weight on such contested economic data. Clearly the stakes were high for the World Bank in terms of seeking out data that would corroborate the positive view of globalization as poverty alleviator. As to China and India, those two large countries accounting for one-third of the world's population, the evidence is equally controversial. Certainly absolute poverty in both countries was reduced in the last quarter of the twentieth century as capitalist modernization took hold of both economies. But there is a huge amount of guesswork in the figures for those countries, especially China, which did not cooperate with international poverty-measurement exercises. Wade concludes: "The lack of reliable price comparisons for India and China—hence the lack of reliable evidence on the purchasing power of incomes across their distributions—

compromises any statement about levels and trends in world poverty" (Wade 2004, 23). So while the social transformation of India
and China is hugely significant, the larger picture is still one in which
the benefits of globalization are very unevenly distributed. Even the
World Bank's revised data that show declining absolute poverty levels in China and India show those living in absolute poverty increasing between 1980 and 2000 for Latin America (up from 48 to 56
million), sub-Saharan Africa (up from 241 to 323 million), the Middle
East (up from 5 to 8 million), and in Eastern Europe and Central
Asia (up from 6 to a staggering 20 million) (World Bank 2004).

So despite the many optimistic readings of globalization in terms
of inequality generation, there is now a growing consensus that it
has essentially increased the level of global inequality over the last
quarter of a century. Perhaps the best place to start is with a broad
review of globalization and growth carried out for the IMF (Crafts
2000). The divergence in income levels and growth rates, which this
study confirmed, contradicted the neoclassical tenet that economic
growth should lead to convergence. This study shows the IMF to
be openly skeptical of OECD future growth projections. In particular, Crafts argues that "sustaining strong catch-up growth performance is seen as rather difficult and dependent on unpredict-
able success in achieving policy reform and institutional innovation
as the economy develops" (Crafts 2000, 52). The Asian crisis of
1997–98 demonstrated that while some third-world national economies can indeed catch up with the developed economies, they could
also fall back. More generally, the IMF understands that there will
not be overall convergence among national economies in the foreseeable future.

If international inequality is not declining as a result of globalization, neither is intra-national income distribution improving, according to a detailed World Bank study (Milanovic 2002). Based uniquely
on household survey data and covering the period from 1988 to 1993,
this study found that during that critical period for the rise of globalization the poorest 5 percent of the world's population lost almost
one-quarter of its income while the top 5 percent gained by 12 percent (Milanovic 2002, 74). The overall picture of global income inequality can best be seen from a United Nations University study
that surveyed seventy-three countries in 2001. It found that while
nine countries (accounting for 5 percent of the total population) had
seen decreasing levels of income inequality when comparing the

1960s with the 1990s, in 48 countries 9 accounting for 59 percent of the population) saw increasing levels of income inequality over the same period, with the balance (sixteen countries and 36 percent of the population) having seen stable levels of inequality (Cornia and Kirski 2001).

We could simply accept that inequality among and within countries has increased with globalization (see, for example, Chossudovsky 2003), but there are serious issues of measurement and conceptualization that we must necessarily consider before arriving at a balanced and sustainable view. As Robert Wade explains, the answer to the question of whether world income distribution is becoming more polarized depends on at least three factors:

- Whether countries are weighted for population (consider China, for example);
- Whether income is compared on the basis of market exchange rates or purchasing-power parity (PPP) rates; and
- Whether we measure inequality through the Gini coefficient or in terms of quintiles distribution (Wade 2001, 14).

Clarifying these measurement and methodological issues is a prerequisite if we are actually going to be talking about the same thing when debating the impact of globalization on patterns of social inequality.

In an important debate around the interpretation of world income inequality Glenn Firebaugh (1999) highlighted the importance of weighting national data in terms of population size. To summarize, as Firebaugh puts it: "When each national economy is given the same weight the data indicates national divergence. Yet weighted studies find stability. . . . So the issue turns of weighting. Do we want to give nations or individuals equal weight?" (Firebaugh 1999, 1604). It may seem obvious from a sociological viewpoint to deal with weighted data but then we may wish, in terms of a theory of imperialism, for example, to compare national economies as units. Furthermore, with population-weighted measures increasing birth rates in poor countries near the mean give the appearance of reducing measured inequality (Babones 2002, 21). Finally, given the problem of deriving comparable data for China, and its weight in terms of global population, there are strong arguments for excluding that country from population-weighted measures of inequality.

A debate related to that on population is that between the proponents of market exchange rates and those who favor PPP. Firebaugh makes a strong case for moving away from the conventional first measure, which converts the local currency to the average exchange rate to the US dollar over the last three years. The PPP method, by contrast, converts national incomes into purchasing power in terms of a comparable bundle of goods and services. This has the practical effect of raising the income levels of the poorer countries. For Firebaugh, PPP is a superior measure because the foreign exchange rate method "is an unreliable method for comparing national incomes" and "the use of official exchange rates exaggerates intercountry inequality" (Firebaugh 1999, 1609). Be that as it may, the PPP measures only go back to the 1970s, and thus long runs are not possible. More fundamental, the PPP approach is not as useful as the previous one in terms of assessing relative nation-state power in the world system or consideration of class conflict on a global scale.

The Gini coefficient has long been the standard measure of income inequality. However, it is well known that the Gini coefficient "tends to overstate changes close to the average and understate changes close to the extreme" (Wade 2001, 6). Given this problem, we obtain a more accurate picture of the extremes by comparing the top quintile (20 percent) or decile (10 percent) with the bottom end of the spectrum. Thus the UNDP neatly encapsulates the nature of global inequality by showing, for example, that the assets of the two hundred richest people in the world are greater than the combined income of 40 percent of the world's people living in poverty (UNDP 1999, 20). The use of averages such as the Gini coefficient does allow us to make comparisons, but such averages cannot capture the stark realities of inequality.

In conclusion, there is now fairly widespread agreement that there are winners and losers in the global economy (see Kapstein 2000). There is also now a generalized understanding that a rising tide does not necessarily lift all boats, as it were. Even those boats that were lifted, such as China, may well not have risen due to globalization but rather due to internal social transformations. Absolute poverty worldwide may have declined since the onset of globalization, but the data are at least controversial. Global inequality levels have actually risen, according to all measure except one, and even that one becomes negative when China is removed from the equation. Overall, then, globalization has not been a poverty and inequality alleviator.

STRUCTURAL ADJUSTMENT

When globalization reached its stride in the 1990s the so-called developing world had already accepted the economic lead of the powerful capitalist Western economies and the failure of alternative development models. Throughout the 1980s many developing countries were forced to accept structural adjustment policies as a condition for obtaining IMF and World Bank loans to surmount the economic crises they were facing. Earlier structural adjustment was the way developing countries met the problems posed by the 1974 oil crisis. The conventional wisdom at the time was that only those countries that had opened their economies to the world system were able to sustain better growth rates in the 1980s. The symptoms of macroeconomic disequilibrium displayed in the rest included a large current account deficit, high inflation rates, and slow or stagnant economic growth. Adjustment, according to the World Bank, had two objectives: "reducing the demand for imports and domestic goods to stabilize economic conditions and restructuring the economy to reach a higher growth path" (World Bank 1990, 103). So how did stabilization and adjustment work out in practice?

The IMF had always imposed conditions on its loans, but after the debt crisis erupted in the South around 1982–83 these conditions become more stringent and formalized. For a while the IMF concentrated on stabilization loans, leaving the World Bank to deal with more long-term structural adjustment programs, but by the late 1980s that distinction had largely eroded. In principle a "stabilization loan" would be granted, conditional on implementation of what became generally known as an austerity plan. Governments would be urged to devalue their currency, cut their budget deficit (usually through trimming the state sector), abolish any price contexts that might exist, and remove any ceilings on interest rates to curb inflation. Then came the structural adjustment loans designed, as Pamela Sparr explains, "to restructure an economy to promote long-term growth and economic efficiency" (Sparr 1994, 7). The changes in public policy were considerable.

What the stabilization and structural programs aimed for was the neoclassical economic objective of "getting prices right." The optimum equilibrium rate would be achieved basically through liberalizing markets and eliminating any state interference in the setting or regulating of prices for products or services. The state was seen as too heavy-handed to get prices right, so it must withdraw from the economy as far as possible, for example, through the privatization of state firms. Another goal of the structural adjustment loans, as Sparr explains, was "to create a more 'open' economy" (Sparr 1994, 8). This entailed not only removing all tariff barriers and any other impediment, legal or otherwise, to the free movement of goods and services, but also, usually, export-oriented growth. This contrasted with the earlier postwar development model of inward (internal market)-oriented growth. As these plans were implemented, their underlying dynamic became evident.

As a response to economic crisis the adjustment programs reflected a logic of sorts, but as a means of moving toward a new growth path they were far from successful. For every East Asian NIC (newly industrializing country) that seemed to make a leap forward, there were other countries for which the programs meant stagnation. One study of World Bank structural adjustment programs in the 1980s across a wide range of countries found that they "did not show any significant impact from such loans on Gross Domestic Product (GDP) growth rates" (Elson 1994, 32). While in the short term the balance of payments might have improved, in the long term investment rates were adversely affected. By exposing the developing country's economy even more to the vagaries of the world market, the sources of instability multiplied. In a major attempt to advance the optimistic scenario it was advocating, the World Bank published a report on sub-Saharan Africa's adjustment and growth in the 1980s (World Bank 1986) arguing that it was possible to go "from crisis to sustainability," but the sharp critical reaction to the selective use of data in this report made the attempt backfire.

Indeed, by the end of the 1980s it was widely recognized that structural adjustment led to widespread deprivation, and there were calls from major international organizations like UNICEF (United Nations Children's Fund) for "adjustment with a human face." For Latin America the 1980s were characterized as the lost decade, as every indicator available for social and economic development stagnated or became worse. The costs of "adjustment" were invariably borne by the poorest households, which were forced to develop survival strategies but often sank further into poverty. As employment in the formal sector shrank, many workers were driven into the informal sectors. For all the talk about protecting the vulnerable by those seeking to "humanize" the process, the fact remained that many households were simply unable to absorb the strains placed on them by structural adjustment.

One of the most noticeable features of the adjustment programs was the particularly deleterious effect it had on women. The household, as Diane Elson reminds us, is "a site of tension and conflict as well as cooperation—a site of inequality as well as mutuality" (Elson 1994, 35). It was women who bore the main brunt of trying to make ends meet, not men. The structural adjustment programs, in their supposedly gender-blind perspective, were actually implementing a male bias consistently and in many ways. By simply ignoring unpaid work—which of course plays a major role in household survival strategies—the World Bank and other agencies made invisible the contribution of women to social reproduction as well as production. The very notion of efficiency that lies at the heart of stabilization and adjustment programs was imbued with a "male" scientific flavor that could not capture any alternative social logic of human development.

The structural adjustment policies of the 1970s continued into the 1990s but took the much more aggressive form of neo-liberal "economic reforms" deemed necessary to fit developing countries into the emerging system of globalization. India with its 687 million inhabitants would provide a key case study in the debate around whether globalization has fostered greater economic equality or inequality. Rapid economic growth in India (as in China) in the 1990s led to a significant decrease in the number of people living in absolute poverty in that country. Indeed, combining India and China we see the main factor explaining the optimistic reading that globalization reduces poverty worldwide. India (much like China) engaged in a controlled and gradual liberalization of the economy, and one detailed econometric study concludes: "There is compelling evidence that the reforms have exacerbated inequality. However, the deterioration in India has been less substantial than that in several transition [to capitalism] economies" (Jha 2000, 25).

India in the 1980s did not suffer from the same degree of inflation, foreign debt, and social inequality that Latin America did. Consequently, stabilization was more readily achieved, and liberalization in the 1990s was launched in a favorable atmosphere. Privatization and reduction of protection tariffs proceeded apart and the fiscal reform was relatively successful. There was even a recognition that many of India's workers existed outside of the market, and measures were taken to minimize the inequality-generating aspects of the reforms. However, as Raghbendra Tha concludes, "in both the rural and the urban sectors, at the all-India level inequality was higher post-reform that it was at the time of the crisis" (Jha 2000, 39). Since inequality in the urban areas was always higher than in the rural areas, and rapid growth leads to migration to the cities, there was a significant increase overall in inequality levels.

At one level it is quite simply a case of a shift in the distribution of income from wages to profits that explains the rise of inequality in India. Rural inequality did not rise as fast as urban inequality, but rural poverty rose markedly as a result of declining rural wages and the withdrawal of state subsidies for food and fertilizers. Regional inequalities among the various states of India also increased markedly. However, it is significant that the states with the highest levels of inequality (as measured by the Gini coefficient) are also those where economic growth has been most sluggish. According to Tha, "this reinforces the view that rapid economic growth remains the best bet for reducing India's immense problems of inequality and poverty" (Jha 2000, 39). But this can be achieved only if further efforts are made "to see that the distribution of consumption does not become further skewed" (Jha 2000, 39). How that might be done is not entirely clear, however, and this is a general weakness in many economistic prescriptions.

The problem is that one can argue that economic growth is a necessary precondition for generating social developments and ameliorating social inequality, but it is not a sufficient condition. We have seen how structural adjustment and the later neo-liberal economic reforms were bound to generate more inequality, even when they were successful in fomenting economic growth. It is simply not enough to call for adjustment with a human face or, as it is now called, globalization with a human face. Such policies at best can deliver only ameliorating measures; at worst they actually seek to make the poor complicit in their own oppression. The politics of inequality (see the section below) can be approached through a complex set of theoretical elaborations, but also in relation to its interaction with state policies and political struggles.

EASTERN CAPITALISM

It can plausibly be stated that neo-liberal globalization—the extension of capitalism across the globe—was only consolidated after the collapse of the Berlin Wall in 1989. This event signaled the end of the alternative development model. The transition countries of Eastern Europe and the former Soviet Union, as they became known, were to be the site of a huge social experiment. The stabilization and structural adjustments that had been deployed over the previous decade in the South were to be applied vigorously and abruptly in the East. The transition to capitalism provides an opportunity, as Simon Clarke writes, "to evaluate those doctrines [of economic liberalism] by assessing the consequences of their application. Success in Russia will surely vindicate the universalistic claims of these doctrines, while failure should send their proponents back to the drawing board" (Clarke 1992, 6). It is precisely such an evaluation that we should attempt now, focused particularly on our overall theme of international integration and national disintegration as the main effects of globalization.

Structural adjustment "without anesthetics" appealed to the Soviet economic reformers, and, of course, their US advisors were more than keen to operate on the corpse of communism. It was seen as a brusque but necessary way of breaking the military and political monopoly of power and the rigidities introduced by a bureaucratic state planning system. However, the net result in the 1990s was a sharp and sustained fall in production, a rise in inflation, and very little to show by way of foreign investment. In the Russian Federation, by far the most populous country in the new Commonwealth of Independent States (CIS), GDP shrank by 40 percent in the course of the 1990s. It is estimated that industrial employment fell by one-third and wages fell by almost two-thirds. But, as the ILO puts it, "the worse aspect of economic restructuring [in the transition countries] is the appalling growth in the number of people living in poverty" (ILO 1995, 111).

While in 1990 one in twenty-five people in the CIS lived in absolute poverty (defined as less than US$2.15 a day), by the end of the decade that number had risen to one in five. In the Soviet Federation, after a bout of severe inflation in 1992, it was actually estimated that 80 percent of the population had incomes that placed them below the poverty line. Women workers were particularly hard hit as they were driven by the new capitalist order back into the domestic sphere. Workers who were lucky enough not to lose their jobs were pushed into precarious, low-income jobs where the concept of a minimum wage seemed a quaint relic of a long-gone past. The welfare state, which was what socialist regimes represented in practice for most workers, was also to become an increasingly patchy affair or simply empty rhetoric about safety nets. Individual survival strategies were no match for a capitalism seeking to recolonize the Eastern countries that had been taken out of its rule.

The World Bank and the other international financial institutions could not fail to recognize the magnitude of the social catastrophe unleashed in many transition countries. They recognized that countries such as Russia passed from having one of the lowest levels of inequality in the world to becoming one of the most unequal, as testified by a Gini coefficient that nearly doubled in the 1990s. However, they generally refuse to accept that liberalization caused this growing inequality that is, instead, put down to corruption and rent-seeking (rather than entrepreneurial) behavior by the new capitalists. What the World Bank effectively argues is that there is "bad" inequality as in Russia and the other CIS states, and a "good" inequality such as that present in Central and Southeastern Europe. For the latter, the Bank argues that "positive developments largely explain the rise in inequality: rising returns to education, decompressing wages, and emerging returns to risk taking and entrepreneurship. These forces are welcome, despite the increase in inequality" (World Bank 2002, xiv).

The argument for welcoming this "good" inequality is that it demonstrates that "the market" is now rewarding "skills and efforts," as well as an ill-defined process of "risk-taking." It is supposedly only the capture of the state by partisan social groups in Russia that has led to a perversion of the reform process. There is certainly an argument to be made around the political context of the various transition processes. However, when in the 1990s market forces were "liberated," the outcome could not be predicted; it would be naive for Western advisors to turn around and express shock over the "gangster capitalism" that emerged in Russia, for example. It is inconceivable to put the failure of the transition down simply to the unintended consequences of the shock therapy administered on IMF advice. As Joe Stiglitz, who was part of this process as senior World Bank economist, explains, "The IMF's focus on macroeconomics— and particularly on inflation—led it to shunt aside issues of poverty, inequality and social capital" (Stiglitz 2002, 161). That is still a generous reading, because it is hard to see the social consequences of the transition regimes as anything but intended from the start to launch a bold new era of primitive capitalist accumulation.

What became quite clear a decade after the transition began in Russia was the primacy of politics in the process. So, for example, while the World Bank still argued for the need to "impose market discipline," it also recognized that "government must be credible and able to constrain oligarchs and insiders" (World Bank 2002, 94). That would require a strong state, and not one liquidated in the interest of allowing market forces free play. It is the discipline of democracy and not that of the market that would be needed to minimize the social disruption and disintegration caused by the transition to market capitalism. What the World Bank does not seem to realize is the contradiction between preaching the virtues of the market, on the one hand, and, on the other hand, arguing for "mobilizing collective action . . . to enhance political competition" and "enhancing political contestability by mobilizing civil society" (World Bank 2002, 111, 114). This would entail a project of radical democratization quite at odds with the neo-liberal program.

China is a special case in terms of the transition to capitalism insofar as it has been carefully managed by a still nominally communist state. It is also an important case because of its huge population and accelerated economic growth in the 1990s lie behind many studies purporting to show a decline of global inequality levels in the era of globalization. The initial market reforms in China were concentrated in the rural sector and did not have a marked effect on income distribution. However, in the second half of the 1980s the market reforms were focused decisively on the urban and individual sectors, and there they had a marked effect on income distribution. By 1995 China was to reach US levels of income inequality, even though it is argued by some that "the pronounced surge on inequality from 1984 to 1995 was dominated by the rise in urban-rural and coastal-hinterland gaps, not by widening gaps within any given locale" (Lindert and Williamson 2001, 32). That is still evidence that capitalist development in China, as elsewhere, is inherently uneven.

The underlying fact behind this argument is that migration to the cities was more or less banned in China before the mid-1990s. So it was the coastal regions and the cities linked to the global economy that forged ahead, leaving behind these restricted to the rural hinterlands. The argument then goes that the problem of growing inequality is not about globalization per se but differential access to the benefits of linking with the global economy. This argument is really a follow-on from an earlier one in development studies in relation to which economist Joan Robinson once allegedly commented, "If there is one thing worse than exploitation, it is not being exploited." That is to say, capitalism is a dynamic process and an exploitative one, but those left out of it will suffer from marginalization. This is an issue we shall return to at various points, but it is flagged here in relation to China, given the sharpness of contradictions in development there.

There is no doubt that China has grown very fast over the last decade, but there are reasons to doubt PPP income has risen from 0.3 of the world average in 1990 to 0.45 in 1998, which would represent a 0.15 rise in less than a decade. According to Robert Wade, the actual annual growth rate in China during the 1990s was closer to 5–6 percent than the 8–10 percent officially claimed (Wade 2001, 18). Some specialists even argue that there may have been no growth overall in the 1990s at all. However, even with a moderate downward adjustment of China's figures, we find the much touted view that globalization has improved worldwide income distribution clearly disproved. Furthermore, if we add into the equation the worsening income distribution within China—testified to by the increase in average income in the richest to the poorest province being 7 to 1 in 1990 to 11 to 1 by the late 1990s—then the alleged reduction in global income inequality becomes totally illusory.

This quick survey of the transition to capitalism in the East leads us to several conclusions. We have witnessed over the last decade a social transformation every bit as profound, and with an even more uncertain outcome, than the original revolutions in the East. After recognizing the great growth in inequality in most transition countries, the World Bank, in a major survey of the lessons of the first ten years of the capitalist counter-revolution, can only suggest somewhat weakly that governments should "focus on closing the gap between winners and losers in the short term" (World Bank 2002, 111). But apart from seeking to lower "the high concentration of gains" for the winners, the Bank can only recommend for the losers "preserving a social safety net that cushions the dislocations of the downsizing state sector" (World Bank 2002, 111). After a decade of transition to a wild unregulated capitalism, encouraged, if not led, by Western "experts," these seem rather lame lessons to be learning. But they are lessons that fed into debates in the late 1990s on the politics of inequality, or to put it more explicitly, what is to be done.

POLITICS OF INEQUALITY

For the UNDP "the fight against poverty is a deeply political issue. Poverty in most societies is about disparities in the distribution of power, wealth and opportunity" (UNDP 2002, 4). These disparities cause conflict, and that conflict must be managed in the interests of global governance. Poverty, and inequality more generally, is once again at the center of attention for international policymakers. These policies have advanced conceptually since the 1970s "trickle down" theories, which assumed that the benefits of structural adjustment would in the long run percolate down through society to benefit the poor. The World Bank and other international financial institutions have, in the intervening period, learned a lot from their critics. Today the "gender proofing" of anti-poverty programs is part of the mainstream of development agencies and the empowerment of the poor is something the World Bank places at the heart of its proclaimed strategy to alleviate poverty.

In its first *World Development Report* for the twenty-first century the World Bank proclaimed the fight against poverty as its main priority (World Bank 2000). It recognizes that there is deep poverty across the world, with almost half of the world's population living on less than US$2 per day, and a fifth living on less than US$1 per day. The Bank argues that it is possible to cut by half those who live in extreme poverty by 2015. These international development goals also include a broader commitment to gender equity and reducing other aspects of human deprivation leading to inequality. This, according to the World Bank, will be achieved through a triple strategy of opportunity, empowerment, and security. Opportunity is to be created by encouraging private investment to create jobs, with international markets in particular being seen as offering "a huge opportunity for jobs and income growth—in agriculture, industry, and services" (World Bank 2000, 8).

It is recognized that if poor or developing countries open up to the world market, this will create losers as well as winners. That is where the issue of security comes in. National programs will have to be developed (it is not quite explained how) to "manage the risk of financial and terms of trade shock" (World Bank 2000, 10). The poor will have to get by with "micro-insurance" programs to match the micro-credit programs already in place. Empowerment, the third leg of the World Bank strategy, involves promoting community development and, above all, promoting gender equity, seen as a way of maximizing economic potential. Finally, the World Bank argues, quite noncontroversially that "social structures that are exclusionary and inequitable, such as class stratification or gender divisions, are major obstacles to the upward mobility of poor people" (World Bank 2000, 10). So, does this mean that the World Bank will set as a priority an attack on exclusionary and inequitable social structures?

In dealing with the transition economies in the 1990s, the international financial institutions faced one of their greatest challenges. While bringing the socialist states back into the capitalist fold was a momentous step, the associated risks were also high. What this decade of transition to capitalism led to was a significant debate on how the risks of global integration leading to social disintegration would be handled. What the World Bank has developed as a bottom-line position is certainly not the need to dismantle inequitable social structures. The key position of the World Bank is that "greater disparity of wages, income, and wealth is—up to a point—a necessary part of transition, because allowing wages to be determined by the market creates incentives for efficiency that are essential for successful reform" (World Bank 1995, 66). So, whatever else is added on in terms of safety nets for the poor, the essential cornerstone of the World Bank's politics of inequality is that market mechanisms are central and sacrosanct.

The politics of inequality today mean that the international financial institutions usually claim to be building "globalization with a human face" and are cognizant of the inequalities attendant on economic globalization (see, for example, UNDP 1999). Since 2000 the World Bank and the IMF have developed a common approach called poverty reduction strategy paper (PRSP) approach. At the core of the PRSP is a hard-line neo-liberal market fundamentalism, but this is packaged within a whole range of participatory techniques designed to "facilitate empowerment." There is now great stress on the need for effective participation by civil society and listening to the voices of the poor. The PRSP, which has rapidly gained influence across the world, is based squarely on a decentralized approach and area-based initiatives such as health action zones and education action zones, where social development is focused on localities.

The PRSP approach is certainly a long way from the trickle-down approach to poverty reduction of the 1970s. It is certainly a more inclusive approach, and it would strenuously oppose all forms of social exclusion, if only because of the economic inefficiency they create. However, as Craig and Porter point out, "Promoting universal social integration, while remaining silent about power issues, PRSP's heighten critics" fears that they serve as an instrument of hegemonic economic interests" (Craig and Porter 2003, 55). That is to say, it promotes inclusion not because of concern for the poor and excluded but rather to prevent the uncontrolled increase of social exclusion and the political risks of instability associated with it. Clearly, the international financial institutions have become more sophisticated in their approach to global poverty. Global governance requires a "softer" approach than that of a naked neo-liberalism, but it is clear that the needs of global economic integration still take precedence.

The problem, however, lies deeper than just the uneasy mix between economic-liberalism and social-welfare approaches. The World Bank and development agencies throughout the world today promote social capital as the new paradigm that will lead to poverty reduction. While it represents a move beyond the economism of the early liberal policymakers, it introduces a whole new set of problems. Social capital, put most simply, focuses on the social networks and community relations that poor people develop. These social networks or capital (in an analogy with cultural capital) can be resources for the poor in dealing with the social disruption caused by neo-liberalism. However, it is unclear precisely how social capital will be developed, or civil society empowered in a worldwide system based essentially on economic concentration and marginalization of the losers in the competitiveness race, whether people or countries.

A major weakness of social capital as an addendum to neo-liberalism is that it does not correct the gender bias of previous mainstream approaches to poverty and inequality. As Maxine Molyneux argues: "A gender-aware approach to social capital has to begin not just by recognizing but also by problematizing the fact that women are very often central to the forms of social capital that development agencies and governments are keen to mobilize in their poverty-relief and community-development programs" (Molyneux 2002, 177). Just as women were expected to carry the extra burden imposed by structural adjustment, they now are being expected to knit their communities together to produce social capital. As a policy agenda the social-capital approach is totally oblivious to gender inequalities and tends, in practice, to reinforce traditional patriarchal structures. This is not to say that some of the principles of social capital might not be useful, but only as part of a more radical agenda for social transformation.

CONCLUSION

This chapter has explored the various aspects of global inequality and poverty in the era of globalization. While some reduction in absolute poverty in the rapidly modernizing contexts of India and China is not contested, the overall optimistic scenario of the globalizers finds little empirical basis. There are methodological disputes that will linger on, but there is also the key issue of what is to be done in relation to poverty and inequality. From a World Bank perspective, Nancy Birdsall argues that "not all inequality is a bad thing. Some inequality represents the healthy outcome of differences across individuals in ambition, motivation and willingness to work" (Birdsall 1999, 1). This "constructive" inequality—seen to be characteristic of "equal opportunity" societies—is contrasted with "negative" inequalities such as those involving access to land or education in Latin America. It is the latter form of inequality that is now beginning to concern the multilateral economic organizations that see its negative long-term impact on economic growth and its role as a direct cause of social instability. From a social-justice perspective, however, we can only read inequality as an aspect of social exclusion that conspires against any project for global justice.

We also found that while the mainstream approaches to inequality seem to rely simply on the magic of the market to ensure a more efficient distribution of resources, the "globalization with a human face" strategy seems to offer little more than a safety net to its unfortunate losers. Nevertheless, the equality agenda is once again firmly on the table for the international political economy. This is so for a number of reasons. In the first place, globalization, with its worldwide dynamic extension of capitalist relations, is creating greater social divergence than ever before. Its results are complex, but overall convergence is certainly not occurring. In the second place, globalization has undermined precisely those institutions, such as the nation-state, and the welfare state that in the whole postwar period ameliorated the forces tending toward social inequality. Today, the promoters of globalization are forced to take up the issue of equity if only from the point of view of stable governance.

Inequality is multidimensional, including not only the economic aspects discussed here but also important political, institutional, and security dimensions. As Hurrell and Woods argue, these dimensions are often played down, "as have the effects of all dimensions of inequality on the practices of world politics" (Hurrell and Woods 1999, 2). It is precisely that combined and uneven development of capitalism through globalization that we must continue to analyze in the chapters to come in order to extend and deepen the approach developed in this chapter. We need to examine how the spaces and places where globalization operates are characterized by exclusion (Chapter 4). Then, we need to deconstruct or unpack the forms of inequality discussed in this chapter by examining their gender (Chapter 5), race (Chapter 6), and class (Chapter 7) dimensions. It is on that basis that we can return to the politics of inequality on a global scale to examine what strategies might be developed to overcome the limitations of the mainstream and also the alternative strategies currently on offer.

4

Global Places / Spaces of Exclusion

Exclusion has a clear spatial dimension as well as a social aspect. Those excluded from the new globalized, informationalized capitalism are not only on the social margins of society but also on the spatial margins, whether in inner-city ghettoes or peripheral countries that do not fully participate in the global economy. Social exclusion is currently being "re-spatialized" as the socially excluded groups or countries refuse to be marginalized. This chapter explores these themes first in relation to the so-called global cities, widely seen as the great success stories of globalization but locations where its social contradictions are also clearly visible. The poor neighborhoods of these and other cities across the globe are then analyzed in terms of the social-exclusion problematic, as are the poor countries that are increasingly excluded, or perversely included, by the globalization machine. Finally, we examine to what extent a global social policy is, or could be, dealing with the social and spatial aspects of social exclusion.

GLOBAL CITIES

The great cities of the world have always been central to the expansion of capitalism across time and space. In the age of empire the colonial cities were the "transmission belts" of metropolitan economic, social, and cultural flows and the hubs of their political and military power in the colonized territories. Today, in the era of globalization, economic internationalization has made the large global city into a key arena for its reproduction and also, I argue, its contestation. Cities became much more open or permeable to global trends in the last quarter of the twentieth century. There are now a number of global cities that operate as veritable command centers of the new global economy and polity. This process is dynamic and has generated massive economic growth in certain places but also has created new and growing social and economic inequalities both within and between the global cities.

Saskia Sassen has usefully defined global cities as "strategic sites in the global economy because of their concentration of command functions and high-level producer-service firms oriented to world markets," or in much broader terms, "cities with high levels of internationalization in their economy and their broader social structure" (Sassen 1999, 154). Whether headquarters of the big transnational corporations or international financial institutions, the stock markets, or even major advertising agencies, we find them clustered in the major Western cities. They host the leading, cutting-edge technology industries and also the main cultural industries. In an information society they are the epicenter of information generation and, not surprisingly, are intensively networked through the World Wide Web. They are the physical site for much of the concentration and accumulation of capital, and they are also key destinations for both domestic and international migrants seeking work. It is clear that New York, Tokyo, and London meet these definitions and are "ideal" global cities.

If the top three global cities are easy to visualize as command centers of the new global informational economy, the rest of the list is more disputed. Many other cities claim to be global in terms of their role in the new financial world order, such as Miami, Los Angeles, Frankfurt, Amsterdam, and Singapore. There are also the "wannabe world cities," those struggling in a highly competitive environment to become modes of the global network of commanding cities. One cannot really exclude from this category the great cities of the South, such as Mexico City and São Paulo, Manila and Seoul, Cape Town and Delhi, and also the second-order cities of the industrialized world such as Toronto, Barcelona, Atlanta, and Sydney, which may increasingly play an intermediation role in the new global economy. In terms of global connectivity and global competitiveness—two key measures of globalization and success within its terms—the list of global cities and those within their constellations or spheres of influence is probably bound to increase in the years to come.

It might be best to move toward a taxonomy of the global city— its definition and its qualifying entrants—to look at the space of flows this phenomena has created and is part of. Castells, in particular, places great emphasis on how "the power of the global city is mobilized through the networks of globalization" (Castells 1996, 410). Emphasis is placed less here on the city as a site or location than on its role in the networks of globalization, which has empowered it and placed it in a strategic node position. It is the flows of finance and information in particular that link the global cities while, at the same time, lessening the links of each global city to its national economy. The links between the big city and its hinterlands, the smaller towns, and the villages of its country have broken down. What we find, instead of the national networks of old, is an international network of urban spaces that is strongly hierarchical imposing itself and mapping itself over the once nationally structured flows of business, culture, and commodities.

If we move beyond conceiving of the global city as a place and examine it more as a process, then we can see how (just like globalization generally) it is structured not only by economic inclusion but also by social exclusion. Castells is quite clear that "what is most significant about mega-cities is that they are connected externally to global networks and to segments of their own countries, while internally disconnecting local populations that are either functionally unnecessary or socially disruptive" (Castells 1996, 401–7). This principle is central to an understanding of the global city. A relational approach stresses to what extent connectivity is matched by a certain disconnectivity, or what we are here calling social exclusion. This dialectic of inclusion/exclusion or connection/disconnection lies at the heart of the contemporary dynamics of globalization. Against all the optimistic readings of globalization leading to economic and social convergence, this perspective stresses, rather, a trend toward social polarization as the inevitable consequence of a competitiveness that is unregulated by social mechanisms.

If globalization in broad terms can be seen to lead to social polarization, then this is inevitably true of the global-city process as well; that is, there is a new hierarchy among cities created by the inexorable drive toward competitiveness in the global economy. It was widely believed in the 1970s that a more balanced urban system would develop in the industrialized countries as the major cities declined in relative terms and secondary cities grew. This tendency was reversed in the era of globalization, however, as uneven development took hold and the major cities became part of the network of global cities. Far from place not mattering in the new information economy, as some analysts have suggested, we have in fact witnessed a reconcentration of economic activities in the big cities as the advantages of agglomeration are realized. A similar pattern can be discerned in most developing countries, where it is easy to see how upwardly mobile people in São Paulo or Johannesburg have more in common with their global-city counterparts than they do with the poor, marginalized, and socially excluded inhabitants of their own country.

Inequality among cities is most stark between those that successfully enter the global-city network—even if in a subordinate role—and those that remain outside it or maybe are displaced from previous leading roles. Some cities might succeed in one phase of the global economy and not in others. It is a bit like the "commodity lottery" that led some developing countries to grow under the imperialist and neo-imperialist world economies while others declined when their main exports dried up or their markets collapsed. Cities now clearly compete with one another (even within one country) on the global market. The dominant urban-regeneration model for declining inner cities or old industrial cities is premised on the need to find a niche market where competitive advantage can be gained. Hence we see a scramble to package or repackage cities across the world to make them more attractive to potential investors. In this crucial competition among cities—"the battle of the growth machines" (Logan and Molotch 1987, 35)—it is not at all clear whether the citizens or communities in these cities actually benefit.

It is within the global cities that we can see most clearly how social polarization has exacerbated old inequalities and created new forms of inequality. The global city contains the cutting edge of the new order but also the worst of the old order (poverty and marginalization), now magnified and made permanent. As part of the globalization drive there has been a large-scale restructuring of the labor process throughout the capitalist economy. Informal, or what some call nontraditional forms of employment, are becoming widespread. Where once there was consensus around stability of employment—if only to ensure a degree of social peace—now the watchword observed everywhere is *flexibility*. What global labor flexibility actually means is a virtual decomposition of the labor force as it becomes fragmented and opened up for exploitation. It is within the global cities—in their streets and back streets over which the high-rise buildings of the financial centers tower—that this phenomena is most pronounced and most decisively affects the immigrant population attracted by these development nodes of contemporary capitalism.

As Saskia Sassen puts it, the global cities "concentrate a disproportionate share of global corporate power and are one of the key
sites for its valorisation. But they also concentrate a disproportionate share of the disadvantage and are one of the key sites for their
devalorisation" (Sassen 1999, xxxiv). In this dynamic process of
growth and growing inequality, a major restructuring of the urban
economy is occurring. The networked financial sector and the information economy as a whole depend on an army of service-sector
workers from secretaries to cleaners, fast-food outlets to auto-repair
shops, all subject to flexibility and a growing informalization of labor relations. The rise of gentrification and expensive housing is
matched by an increase in the number of homeless people in most
big cities. While the new growth sectors are now able to generate
huge profits in the speeded-up world of globalization, the more traditional service sectors, not to mention manufacturing, while they
may be necessary to the lives of citizens, are no longer so profitable
and sink into decay.

Globalization—and the global city phenomena in particular—has
created a far greater degree of social polarization at the local level
than existed in the heyday of the nation-state and industrial capitalism, which, for all their faults, had some tendencies toward the incorporation and inclusion of citizens. While globalization has led to
a more uneven development, it has also generated a new regionalism
and a new localism that may yet help knit together a social and political alliance to meet human needs at the local level; it is only at the
local level that the global city becomes effective and "realizes" itself, as it were. The global city is thus not only a place—a site in
strategic global circuits—but also a contested social space where the
"politics of place" take priority and become the axis for a new dynamic urban politics. To understand that process of contestation—in
all its social, cultural, gendered, and racial complexity—we need to
turn to the poor neighborhoods of the contemporary city, those sites
of multiple forms of disadvantage and structural social exclusion.

POOR NEIGHBORHOODS

The global city is a site of social difference and growing polarization. It is in the city that the spatiality of social exclusion is most
clearly manifested. It is in the poor neighborhoods of the contemporary city that we can see most clearly the economic, political, and
cultural effects of social exclusion. It is also in these neighborhoods

that we can see how globalization is realized at the local level. Michael Porter, guru of the competitive-city model, recognizes in this regard that competitive advantage "is created and sustained through a highly localised process" (Porter 1990, 19). In that competitive process there are winners and losers among cities but also within cities as some areas prosper and others become a concentrated focus for multiple forms of deprivation and exclusion. These neighborhoods include the black inner-city ghettoes of the United States, the French North African *banlieues*, the run-down de-industrializing inner cities of the North, and the shanty towns of the big cities in Latin America, Asia, and Africa.

If the United States is unquestionably the world's leading economy in the era of globalization, its inner-city ghettoes are also one of the clearest manifestations of how unequal that process is. Throughout the 1990s much was made of the dynamism of the free-market system and its capacity to generate more jobs, in contrast to the supposedly more corporatist European model of capitalism. However, this expansion of low-paid, mainly service-sector jobs did nothing to prevent an increasing number of people falling into poverty in the 1980s and 1990s. In fact, much of the "new poverty" emerged precisely among those earning wages below the poverty line. One particularly dramatic manifestation of this accelerating inequality was the growth of homelessness in the United States, which reached somewhere between five and nine million people in the 1990s. It can be argued, as Castells does, "that the social economic, and housing conditions in most inner-city ghettoes have considerably worsened over the past three decades, in spite (or because?) of a sustained effort in urban social programs and welfare policies" (Castells 1996, 137). This process is also and fundamentally, of course, a racial one.

As Massey and Denton note: "For urban blacks [in the United States], the ghetto has been the paradigmatic residential configuration for at least eighty years" (Massey and Denton 1993, 18). What has changed in recent years is the extent to which the urban ghetto has become not just a space of exploitation and domination but also a place of exclusion. It is no longer simply a question of inequality seen as some kind of linear continuum. Today's black and Latino ghettoes in the United States are characterized by a structural form of social exclusion, embedded economically, politically, and culturally. This is "the *abandoned city*, the city of the victims, left for the poor, the unemployed, the excluded" (Marcuse 1996, 196). African Americans in the United States, North Africans in the French *banlieu,* and Turkish *gastarbeieter* in Germany are all subject to this new form of social exclusion as well as the old forms of racism or xenophobia.

Racial discrimination and spatial segregation go hand in hand to produce the ghetto of the excluded. With upwardly mobile black workers and employees moving out of the ghetto, it has become an even more concentrated expression of poverty and social exclusion. William Julius Wilson estimates that high-poverty neighborhoods (defined as those with more than 40 percent of residents living in poverty) increased by 92 percent between 1970 and 1990, with eight million people now living in high-poverty inner-city areas (Wilson 2000, 29). The changing structures of the labor market—with an emphasis on higher levels of education—have exacerbated that process of segregation. This job mismatch is compounded by a lack of affordable housing outside the ghetto. This vicious cycle is then compounded by high crime rates, stigmatization, and political marginalization. It is probably not too far-fetched to see the US inner-city ghetto as a portent for the future of globalization and social exclusion if a strong drive toward social regulation of the free market does not materialize.

In Europe the decline of the industrial city has also had a marked social effect of segregation and disadvantage. The long-term decline in manufacturing and port-based economies has had a devastating impact on many cities for many years, but it has been intensified and seemingly made irreversible by the impact of neo-liberal globalization and the pressures it has placed upon these cities. A negative process of economic transformation thus leads to social dislocation. We can see this dramatically in a city like Liverpool, where the population declined by half between the Second World War and the turn of the century. It is not surprising, in this context, that Liverpool today epitomizes inner-city problems in Britain and has been the recipient of virtually every UK and EU regeneration scheme since the 1980s. While some regeneration has occurred though the leisure and entertainment industries, overall the problem of structural decline has proven intractable. Not surprisingly, when a UK Urban Competitiveness Index was constructed in 2002, Liverpool was found to be the country's "least productive" city. With an unemployment rate double the national average and a mean income only three-quarters of the national level, Liverpool is a stark reminder that there are losers as well as winners in the globalization game, even within the restricted realm of British cities.

It is, then, not surprising to see that a city like Liverpool has a strong clustering of neighborhoods in which poverty and social exclusion are dominant (see Andersen, Munck, et al. 1999; Munck 2003). As Anne Power puts it, more generally, "we have not just created poor neighborhoods, but whole swathes of cities dominated by exclusionary problems" (Power 2000, 4–5). The decline of traditional industry and the negative impact of long-term structural unemployment have decimated many inner-city neighborhoods. Traditional social structures and relationships, such as those of family, church, trade unions, and the work place, have declined in effectiveness in these neighborhoods. What is emerging is a form of dualism between these disconnected or marginal neighborhoods and those linked into the new information economy and globalization. While targeting the worst areas with various social and economic regeneration programs has led to a certain amelioration of deprivation, it is difficult to envisage a solution emerging locally to what is essentially an effect of the exclusionary dynamic of global capitalism.

One of the most enduring concepts to emerge from both the US and European experiences of urban social exclusion is that of an underclass. The term *underclass* originated in the United States as the New Right of the 1980s sought to present welfare recipients as suffering from a "culture of dependency" from which they needed to be weaned if social exclusion was to be overcome. In the version developed by Charles Murray, the term *underclass* reflected a veritable cultural "disease" among the poor "whose values are contaminating the life of entire neighbourhoods" (Murray 1990, 23) through their rejection of work and family ethics. Not all the poor were deemed part of the underclass in this contemporary recasting of nineteenth-century distinction between the deserving and the undeserving poor. Rejecting this charged conservative usage of the term, Wacquant and Wilson argued that "if the concept of underclass is used, it must be a structural concept: it must denote a new socio-spatial patterning of class and racial domination. . . . It should not be used to designate a new breed of individuals moulded freely by a mythical and all powerful culture of poverty" (Wacquant and Wilson 1989, 25).

The term *underclass* is no more precise than earlier terms such as *marginal* or *dangerous* classes. It does seem to capture, though, something of the unprecedented nature of structural social exclusion. We can follow the shift from *working class* through *lower class* to *underclass* as a means to understand how society has changed in the last twenty years or so. The working class was part of a society where class was the structuring element and all classes had a useful function, albeit hierarchical. With the notion of lower class, analysis shifted to the perceived social mobility of the 1950s; those in the lower class may have been at the bottom of the scale, but there was a ladder they could climb. Finally, as Bauman puts it, the term *underclass* "belongs to the imagery of a society which is not all embracing and comprehensive" (Bauman 1998, 66). Society is now decentered, and class is no longer its defining principle. The underclass thus reflects a society in which social groups or categories are excluded—deemed ultimately to be beyond or outside class and society as a whole.

Finally, the urban process of social exclusion provides us with a veritable laboratory to assess the various measures taken to combat social exclusion. A thriving industry has emerged focused on urban regeneration and social exclusion. There is now an integrated approach to sustainable improvement of poor neighborhoods. This includes, according to a 1998 Joseph Rowntree Foundation survey:

- bringing residents to the center of regeneration through buildings skills and enhancing confidence;
- strengthening communities through community capacity-building;
- developing a clear neighborhood focus for services though partnerships.

The key word here is "partnerships," which became the main mechanism for economic and social regeneration in the 1990s; the key underlying concept of this discourse is that of social capital. Local partnerships usually involve the public, private, and voluntary or community sectors. Partnership is seen as central to the new urban policy, but it is unclear to what extent it will affect social exclusion by generating redevelopment or whether it is simply "modernizing" the structures of local government.

The problem for poor neighborhoods, as for poor countries, resides in the nature of the competitiveness in the era of globalization, which has exacerbated previous hierarchies, not lessened them. What has emerged in many cities are "urban growth coalitions" (see Logan and Molotch 1987) committed to a policy of "boosterism." Competition among cities seems to be almost as important as competition among businesses as the city becomes a "growth machine" committed to boosting its local fortunes against other cities both abroad and nationally. It is doubtful, though, if this struggle actually benefits citizens even of the cities that are winners. The policies adopted to carve out a niche in the global economy are often socially regressive and environmentally destructive. They are based on a "beggar thy neighbor" approach that can only be detrimental in the long run. It is the parameters of competitiveness that ultimately set the limits to a partnership approach to combat social exclusion, which seems to end up as simply seeking community support for the growth machines that are pitting city against city.

POOR COUNTRIES

The immensely productive but inequality-generating process of globalization produces poor countries as well as poor neighborhoods. From the era of colonialism onward, large parts of the world were exploited by the dominant rich Western nations. In the classical age of imperialism, which was consolidated in the last quarter of the nineteenth century, an unequal international division of labor was created by force. It provided immense benefits to the North—in the form of cheap labor, cheap inputs for their industries, and a market—but led to underdevelopment in the South. Following the Second World War formal independence was gained by most of the colonies but the United States, as the new dominant power, created a new imperialism based on economic rather than political power. In the 1970s and 1980s" there was an attempt in the South to create a more equitable new international economic order. This initiative came too late, and by the last quarter of the twentieth century the dominant economic powers, led by the United States, had forged a new world order based on US economic and military supremacy.

At first it seemed that if the "correct" economic development strategy was followed, the poor countries of the world could escape from the colonial division of labor and at least join the ranks of the less developed rich nations. Nowhere were these hopes raised higher than in Southeast Asia, where the so-called Tiger economies of South Korea, Taiwan, Hong Kong, and Singapore seemed to be following the example of Japan in forging a developed economy. From the mid-1970s onward these countries developed an export-oriented industrializing strategy with considerable success. It seemed that a new international economic order could indeed be constructed, albeit under the conditions of authoritarian political rule that prevailed in much of East Asia. It was a strategy that was pointed to in Latin

America as proof that there was nothing inevitable about dependency. Once-poor countries could now develop through outward-oriented industrialization, carving out markets for themselves in the global economy. Eventually political democratization and an undoubted improvement in living standards for most of the population silenced the critics who had argued that the model only worked through repression.

Up until the mid-1990s the seemingly spectacular performance of the East Asian economists—replicated at least partly in countries such as Malaysia and Indonesia—was a powerful argument in favor of neo-liberal globalization. However, the 1997 collapse of many major Asian economies, starting with Thailand, was a serious blow to the hegemony of financial liberalization. As Joseph Stiglitz, then with the World Bank, put it: "It is no accident that the two large developing countries spared the ravages of the global economic crisis [of 1997]—India and China—both had capital controls" (Stiglitz 2002, 125). It was the IMF policies themselves—based on financial liberalization and economic stabilization—that brought the world to the verge of economic meltdown. At the turn of century it seemed clear that the East Asian "miracle" had not been based on simple neo-liberal policies; for example, the state had played a major role in economic development. For the developing world as a whole, the prospects were for slow economic growth, at best, with most experiencing declining per capita income.

If the success stories of East Asia were now being called into question, other parts of the developing world were even less successful in escaping underdevelopment. Sub-Saharan Africa, for example, seemed condemned to a form of continental social exclusion as a direct result of the processes of globalization. It would seem that if people or regions do not serve the project or "machine" of free-market capitalism, then they become "surplus to requirements." The sprawling urban slums in the Third World are another case in point. As Davis notes, "At the end of the day, a majority of urban slum-dwellers are truly and radically homeless in the contemporary international economy" (Davis 2004, 26). This is social exclusion in the strongest possible sense of the word, insofar as there is no conceivable way out of the situation. That is not to say that the international economic agencies do not offer a strategy, but it is simply the same one recommended for those people locked into urban deprivation, mainly better education and training so as to find a job.

To those who hold that globalization simply has not gone far enough in sub-Saharan Africa, Castells quite rightly points out that "Africa is not external to the global economy" (Castells 1998, 91). International economic relations have penetrated deeply into the continent, disrupting preexisting patterns of production and consumption. From this perspective it is hard to distinguish between exclusion and exploitation, because clearly the two can go hand in hand. It is not an absolute lack of integration within the world system from which Africa suffers, but the historical legacy of colonialism overlaid by the current patterns of neocolonialism that create a subordinate and disadvantaged insertion into the world system. The politics of social exclusion on a continental scale also lie behind the continuous tragedies of famine and civil war that beset this region (see Duffield 2001).

Since the early 1980s the dominant economic proposal for sub-Saharan Africa has been structural adjustment programs. The evidence of twenty years of these reform efforts shows that they have been unsuccessful in terms of economic development and combating poverty, which still runs at over 50 percent of the population. The latest variant of economic reform is the New Africa Initiative launched in 2001. Sponsored by post-apartheid South Africa, this initiative rapidly gained some international credibility. While accepting the fundamentals of neo-liberal globalization, the New Africa Initiative seeks an African "renaissance" through amelioration of the most negative features creating social exclusion. It has been welcomed as a safe reformist agenda by those in the West who understand the need to regulate economic internationalization, if only for the sake of political stability. The main criticism of this proposal is that it "serves the interests of externally oriented fractions within key (relatively developed) African states while leaving the rest of the continent to sink or swim, as it were, in the globalization current" (Taylor and Nel 2002, 165). At most, South Africa and one or two other countries could enter the turbulent waters of self-regulating international market competition; the rest would sink without a trace.

If sub-Saharan Africa shows how embedded inequality and exploitation is in the world system, there is a new phenomenon where, at a national level, a new poor country is emerging as a direct result of neo-liberal globalization. The most dramatic example is Argentina, which after a decade of rigorous application of IMF recipes went into economic meltdown at the end of 2001. Dianne Abbott, a

British Labour MP, was moved to declare: "Argentina is an extreme example of what happens when a country is run for foreign investors and not for local people. . . . Globalization does not solve poverty. It creates poverty and social chaos. . . . More globalization will mean more Argentinas" (Abbott 2001, 1). The story is more complicated than this, but in essence the statement captures the significance of the case. Toward the end of 2001 Argentina entered a paroxysm of economic, social, and political collapse, which was practically unprecedented. The largest debt default in history (US$155 billion) followed, but this was but a symptom of a deeper crisis for a country that at the end of the 1990s was one of the ten richest countries in the world.

Since 1999 Argentina had followed to the letter the IMF strategy for structural adjustment and stabilization, following a destructive period of hyperinflation. Keen to shake off any lingering "thirdworldist" politics, the government became an unconditional supporter of the United States. It launched the most wide-scale privatization program of the decade and even pegged the peso to the US dollar. The opening of the economy to the world economy proceeded apace as transnational corporations took over the commanding heights of the economy. Not surprisingly, throughout the 1990s Argentina was favored as a locale to invest in by global financial "hot money" players keen to make a quick profit. The public sector was dismantled, and the poorer provinces of the interior began to lose heavily in the "survival of the fittest" atmosphere of the time. By the end of the decade the economy was in recession, the foreign debt was mounting, and exports were not competitive due to the link with the dollar. The crisis, when it came, was not unexpected, but its ramifications are still being felt today. What is at stake in Argentina is the continued viability of the IMF strategy for economic development and what alternatives might emerge (see Munck 2001-2002). It is no exaggeration to state that the collapse of Argentina is as significant to the capitalist globalization project as the collapse of the Berlin Wall was to the socialist project.

The phrase *poor neighborhoods* hardly does justice to the huge sprawling urban slums that constitute the norm for urban living in poor countries that can hardly be described as developing. They represent the future for globalization as much as any promise that developments in China might hold out for a dynamic capitalist future. To draw on a recent, unprecedented, and dramatic study by the UN's Human Settlements Program: an urban slum is defined as a concentrated social/spatial site of social exclusion characterized by low sanitary and environmental conditions, lack of regular land ownership, and a general sense of socio-economic isolation (UN-Habitat 2003). We need to understand that 85 percent of future urban growth will occur in the developing world: the mega-cities of the near future will be Mumbai, Lagos, São Paulo, Jakarta, and Shanghai, not Western cities. It is in these cities that urban slums are providing a portent of massive social exclusion to come. The UN study recognizes that "slums are most obviously related to insufficient social and economic development" but also, against the neo-liberal faith, argues that "what is not too clear is the relationship between sound financial performance and slum reduction, whereby successful macro-economic strategies in poor countries do not necessarily lead to poverty alleviation" (UN-Habitat 2003, 27). This verdict essentially breaks the conceptual link between "sound" economic management and "sound" social consequences. In practice this means that slums will continue to grow and proliferate. What is most dramatic in the findings, though, is that in 2001 more than 920 million people (nearly one-third of the total world urban population) lived in slums (UN-Habitat 2003, 30). That represented 78 percent of the population of the "least developed" category of countries and 43 percent of the developing countries' population. In sub-Saharan Africa 70 percent of the population lives in the unsanitary, precarious conditions of slum dwellings, with that proportion rising to an unbelievable 99 percent in Ethiopia and 94 percent in Mozambique. For the World Bank, the urban slums of the South are a product of "bad governance," but for the UN study they are clearly an inevitable result of neo-liberal globalization. The "challenge of the slums" as raised by the United Nations has not been met by either national or international interventions. With urban poverty set to reach 50 percent of the global urban population by the year 2020, according to the UN study, social exclusion on the scale of the slums is bound to have catastrophic social effects.

GLOBAL SOCIAL POLICY

Across the developing world a new strategy for economic development emerged at the turn of the century. Particularly noticeable is how similar it is to that developed for the poor neighborhoods of the North. It recognizes that structural adjustment has been unduly stringent and harsh in its social effects. It is a strategy that can be called "trickle down plus," following Stiglitz (2002, 80); it sees economic growth as central but adds on some commitment to health and female-education needs in particular. As with the inner-city regeneration programs, the core social and political aspect of the new strategy is the ill-defined concept of partnership. James Wolfensohn, president of the World Bank, writes in this regard that holistic sustainable development will require partnership: "Let's start with the governments of the [developing] countries, and if they don't have adequate capacity, let's help them. Let's deal with the multilaterals and the bilaterals; let's deal with civil society and the private sector" (Wolfensohn 2003, 1). This conception of partnership certainly shows a keen awareness of how contemporary "network society" (Castells 1996) works and the need for good governance. However, it is not clear why a partnership arrangement, say with groups within civil society, would benefit the poor. And even education, clearly a human goal in all cases, might just deliver (as they say in Liverpool) "better educated dole [unemployed] queues." The fact is that even "globalization with a human face" deals with poverty and inequality in a technocratic way. There is a new social agenda creeping into even the IMF discourse, and it is being brought to the fore at the World Bank. However, as a UNRISD report argues: "A single-minded focus on poverty reduction, without broader commitment to improving the quality of life throughout society, obscures issues of income distribution and social equity" (UNRISD 2000, 2). Targeting resources to have an impact on poor people or the poorest countries is simply no substitute for a global social policy, an issue to which we now turn.

Globalization, and the social exclusion it either reproduces or generates, has created the objective need for a global social policy thus "globalizing" traditional social policy (as academic subject and state intervention) intended to improve human welfare through education, health, housing, and social security. The parameters of the nation-state—which from 1944 to around 1975 defined the purpose of social policy—were once unquestioned as the natural basis on which social incorporation into the capitalist project would occur. Even through our cursory examination of how poor neighborhoods and poor countries are generated by neo-liberal globalization, we can see to what extent the determinants of social policy are today mainly, or at least in part, set by global developments. An interesting point is that made by Bob Deacon: "The other side of the coin of the globalization of social policy is the socialization of global politics"

(Deacon, Hulse, and Stubbs 1997, 3). That is to say, the international financial institutions, and the "managers" of globalization more generally, cannot today ignore the social context and social consequences of their economic policies.

Globalization has exacerbated the long-running challenge of social and economic development in the South, but it has also sharpened, through its neo-liberal policies, the crisis of the welfare state in the more affluent countries of the North. In the course of the 1990s a series of major United Nations conferences or world summits marked a new internationalization of social policy. Thus in 1990 we saw the World Summit for Children, in 1992 the UN Conference on Environment and Development, and in 1995 the Fourth World Conference on Women and the World Summit for Social Development. Five years after the 1995 conference at Copenhagen, it was possible to draw a sober balance sheet of how much had changed and what had remained the same in terms of globalization's ability to tackle the problems of social exclusion and the need for social development.

For Bob Deacon, writing in 2000, "international development cooperation appears to have moved a long way from the days of structural adjustment programs advocated by the [World] Bank and IMF with no concern for their short-term negative social consequences" (Deacon 2000, 18). It is undoubtedly the World Bank that has undergone the most significant makeover since the mid-1990s. Even a cursory glance at the Bank's website shows an almost overwhelming focus on "engendered development," "empowerment," "pro-poor growth," and the need to build "social capital." Nevertheless, there have been limits to this turn. In 2000 the US government secured the resignation of Ravi Kanbur, lead author of the *World Development Report* on poverty, and Joseph Stiglitz is now an ex-vice president and chief economist of the Bank. While undoubtedly the Bank sees the flaws in practice (as well as in theory) of an unregulated free-market economic strategy, its concern with building safety nets for the victims of globalization is somewhat negated by making them fundamentally reliant on private-sector-style risk-management strategies.

It is from within the broad family of UN bodies—from the ILO to WHO, from UNICEF to UNESCO—that we see most clearly a growing concern with the social impact of globalization. It was the UNDP that promoted most assiduously the objective of "globalization with a human face" in its publications in the late 1990s (see UNDP 1999).

For the UNDP, the benefits of globalization would only be reaped in the context of stronger governance structures being put in place to promote human rights and the need for greater equity at all levels. Its concern for a sustainable future for globalization makes this a reformist organization, but it still argues unambiguously for the essentially liberating potential of globalization. The development of this "softer" focus on globalization is reminiscent of the development of the human-relations approach to factory work in the 1930s to temper the rigors of the Fordist assembly line. While the latter ruled supreme in terms of the organization of work, the human-relations personnel operated in a sense as maintenance crews for the human "machinery" that operated the line.

While a new, more reformist concern with social policy might be articulated in the global corridors of power, it is doubtful if the economic fundamentals have actually changed. Nothing has happened since the protests at Seattle in 1999 to deflect the WTO in a fundamental way from its course of action. Indeed, the onward march of liberalization has even been extended to public and social services once considered sacrosanct. The Millennium Round of trade negotiations designed to extend free trade into the arena of services has been fraught with difficulties, but the overall trajectory is still clear. Health care, education, water provision, and any other service deemed essential to human welfare will steadily become subject to the dictates of the free (unregulated) market. The WTO's panacea for the developing world is a promise to improve the South's access to the North's markets, still in many areas covered by protectionist measures. Any concern expressed over the social impact on once-regulated markets is always overridden by the commitment to the perceived higher objective of free trade as an uncontested human good.

The IMF remains the key international organization standing firm on the orthodox terrain of stabilization and adjustment, notwithstanding superficial concessions to the Bank's more "caring" discourse. While the IMF did adjust its policies for a while after the East Asian crisis in 1997–98, it was back in full-fledged orthodox mode when it presided over the slow-motion collapse of Argentina in 2001. The IMF still advocates austerity and will only provide loans when clearly contractionary measures such as raising taxes and interest rates, cutting deficits, and searching public expenditure are pursued. Throughout, the IMF has laid stress on macroeconomic policies that might be beneficial in terms of paying a country's creditors, but which are totally counterproductive in terms of generating economic development.

As Stiglitz concludes: "The IMF's focus on macroeconomics—and in particular on inflation—led it to shunt aside issues of poverty, inequality, and social capital. When confronted with this myopia of focus, it would say "Inflation is especially hard on the poor." But its policy was not designed to minimize the impact on the poor" (Stiglitz 2002, 161). That, of course, is the bottom line.

It is necessary now to stand back and evaluate the impact and the limitations of a global social policy. The first thing that becomes clear is that even the most enlightened social reformers of "actually existing globalization" still cling to a positive view of the pure model. Thus Joseph Stiglitz writes that "globalization can be a force for good. . . . Globalization has helped hundreds of millions of people at a higher standards of living. . . . The globalization of the economy has benefited countries which took advantage of it. . . . But for millions of people globalization has not worked" (Stiglitz 2002, 248). The problem is that the implications of that very last sentence might simply overwhelm the alleged benefits in practice. I do not underestimate for one moment the difference between a Joseph Stiglitz and a red-blooded promoter of naked neo-liberalism, but it is still necessary to make explicit that his motive is to reform the system, because "without reform, the backlash that has already started will mount and discontent with globalization will grow" (Stiglitz 2002, 248–49). Maybe "another" more democratic and distributionary globalization is indeed possible, though one might ask why we have seen no signs of its appearance as yet.

The other main flow of the global social-policy discourse centers on its particular political and epistemological origins. If we turn to a recent textbook entitled *Globalization and Human Welfare* (George and Wilding 2002), we see a treatment of the issues that is imbued with the ethics and politics of the British welfare state, complete with quotations from Beveridge and other worthy founders of the postwar British welfare state. Not only is this a highly ethnocentric approach, which assumes that British social democracy, "scaled up," as it were, to deal with globalization, is adequate for today's world, but it also ignores the extent to which the welfare-state model has ever been relevant to the majority world. While the "right to a minimum wage" is certainly a worthwhile objective, it is probably as relevant or realistic in the South as Rosa Luxembourg's famous critique of the "right of nations to self-determination" in which she compares it to the "right" of someone sleeping under a bridge to eat off silver plates.

There are various ways in which we can take the debate beyond that posed by the institutionalist concerns of the mainstream global-social-policy promoters. The growing concern with global governance (variously defined and acted upon) must be a welcome advance on the naked neo-liberalism of the 1980s. However, as deployed by the World Bank, the UN, the ILO, and even the major international NGOs, it has a distinctly institutionalist flavor, and with the WTO and IMF, the term seems designed to coopt or deflect criticism rather than to reform. Furthermore, one could argue that this approach, even when articulated by progressive thinkers such as Bob Deacon, reflects the institutionalist bias of academic social policy that not only privileges state institutions but also, as Nicola Yeates notes, it brings into the equation only "the more institutionalized sectors of opposition movements" (Yeates 2001, 130). There is, however, a much wider and "wilder" process of contestation going on across the globe in relation to the social impact of globalization. It is these "globalization from below" initiatives that are shaping global social policy every bit as much as the policies of enlightened reformers in the international forums.

CONCLUSION

This chapter has allowed us to "spatialize" globalization and its effects on social exclusion. Globalization is not "out there" in some abstract sense but here and there in specific places where it is planned, implemented, and contested. We have surveyed the great global cities, those motors of globalization and at the same time sites of debilitating social exclusion. It is now clear that globalization may generate much wealth, but it also creates poor countries (in the South and what was the East) and poor neighborhoods (in the North). The most poignant and dramatic signal for the future must be the huge urban slums that dominate the social prospects for millions of people across the world. There is now wide recognition not only in UN-related circles but also within the "iron triangle" (the WTO, IMF, and World Bank) that something must be done. Hence the debates on how to develop a global social policy that seeks to find reform strategies to deal with the "downside" of globalization.

In the chapters to come we "unpack" the notions of social exclusion and inequality to trace out their impact in terms of gender (Chapter 5), race (Chapter 6), and class (Chapter 7). These are complex and clearly interrelated divisions, but they allow us to specify more clearly the social dynamics at play. It is on that basis that we can proceed to a proper consolidation of a global social policy "beyond" social exclusion (Chapter 8). John Clarke has set us on this path by reminding us that "globalization implies looking at established questions in social policy in new ways" (Clarke 2000, 214). Globalization has ruptured the traditional unity of nation, state, and welfare. It has posed the politics of scale in an entirely new way, as a complex configuration of local, national, regional, and international levels of intervention provides both challenges and possibilities for social contestation. In contesting social exclusion and inequality at a global scale, we shall seek to go beyond palliative action aimed at inclusion to develop a new active conception of citizenship for the complex era in which we live.

5

Gender and Global Inequality

Neither the development of globalized informational capitalism nor the diverse forms of social exclusion can be approached in a gender-neutral manner. Even in critical international political economy, as Peterson notes, "there is a 'deafening silence' on gender" (Peterson 2003, 26). This chapter addresses the gendered manners in which globalization has affected social exclusion. The first section addresses the different way women have been incorporated into the new informational mode of capitalism as highly paid information workers and as low-paid care workers. We find that globalization has actually exacerbated the social distance between women worldwide. A second section deals with the so-called feminization of poverty as structural adjustment and stabilization have increased the burden on poor women. We then turn to an extreme but revealing facet of gender politics in the new world economy, namely, the global sex trade that has led to the "commodification" of women's bodies. Finally, a fourth section engages with the project of a global feminism seen as a way of empowering women worldwide and eradicating gender-based inequalities.

WOMEN AND INFORMATIONAL CAPITALISM

The new capitalism that began to emerge in the 1980s was based much more on the service sector than on traditional manufacturing (at least in the North), which was declining. The male manufacturing worker was no longer typical, if he ever was in any real sense. The growth sectors of the advanced countries were more likely to be employing women in "post-industrial" occupations. This particular shift of the 1980s was overlaid on the long-term increase in the proportion of women in the paid labor force. In the rich OECD countries the overall participation rate (in paid employment) for women rose from 48 percent in 1973 to 62 percent in 1993. As Castells explains: "The massive entry of women into the paid labor force is due, on the one hand, to the informationalization, networking, and globalization of the economy; on the other hand, to the gendered segmentation of the labor market taking advantage of specific social conditions of women to enhance productivity, management control, and ultimately profits" (Castells 1997, 159–62). In its expansive phase as much as in its downswings, capitalism is a gendered mode of production. This is an important point because gender is too often taken to mean simply "women" when in reality it is a mode of structuring capitalism that affects all members of society. Gender hierarchies (patriarchy, in a word) are a crucial component in capitalism's current expansive phase. Globalization as manifestation of that phase is inextricably bound up with "masculine" notions of penetration (by MNCs, for example, in developing countries) and a forthright macho culture of survival of the fittest in the unregulated market economy it is founded upon on.

So capitalist expansion into a new, more advanced mode based on knowledge and information placed a premium on non-manual skills and benefited women, who had steadily advanced in the educational field. This expansion of capitalism also occurred horizontally, as it were, with capitalist relations of production spreading worldwide. The labor market had, of course, always been segmented in terms of both gender and race. This segmentation occurred in the context of preexisting gender divisions in society that created a subordinate role for women. Thus a 1980s Malaysian investment brochure argued for the benefits of female employment in the following terms: "The manual dexterity of the Oriental female is famous the world over. Her hands are small and she works fast with extreme care. Who, therefore, could be better qualified by nature and inheritance to contribute to the efficiency of a bench-assembly production line than the Oriental girl?" (cited in Elson and Pearson 1981, 149). Of course, her "nimble fingers" were/are socially and culturally constructed.

Globalization, then, can be said to have benefited some women. The gap between well-paid Western male professional workers and their female counterparts has closed to some extent. Notwithstanding the "glass ceiling" with regards to the promotion of professional women, the situation is unrecognizable compared to a century ago or even twenty-five years ago. The rise of Western feminism from the 1970s onward has helped consolidate this advance. In terms of legislation, equal pay and equal access to employment are now universally accepted—if not always implemented. In the South the new international division of labor emerging in the 1970s led to a sustained (if uneven) process of industrialization, from the "world factories" of East and South Asia to the massive new industrial sectors of Brazil, Mexico, India, and China. In most of these cases women were a major component and in some cases (such as the electronics world factories) the majority of the workers entering the industrial world. Did this signal an end to the traditional gender division of labor in contemporary capitalism?

At one level the patriarchal Western family has been in crisis for at least twenty or thirty years. The massive incorporation of women into the paid labor force has exacerbated that crisis. The male breadwinner model sustaining a nuclear family is no longer tenable. With the rise of dual wage-earner families and of female-headed households this model has become a distant memory for most trade unionists. However, there is another tendency—namely, the crisis of the welfare state created by neo-liberalism's privatization drive—which has reinforced traditional gender rules. The general tendency across the North to reduce social services has affected women most severely. The care of young children, the elderly, and the sick is privatized (made profitable), and when families cannot access these services, it is women who resume their traditional caring roles. So whereas some tendencies of contemporary capitalist development have challenged the patriarchal order, others have reinforced the traditional gendered division of labor and disempowered women.

The social transformations unleashed by globalization have led to a reconfiguring of the public/private divide in society. The market has now moved into the once private domain of the household, affecting caring work through privatization. This has exacerbated the traditional silence in citizenship theories focused on the public/private domain, whereby the latter is largely ignored. The current tendency to dissolve the public/private distinction as the whole of society becomes "marketized" also questions the very notion of citizenship. One response to the feminist argument for an "engendered" conception of citizenship is that of David Marquand (1991), who considers it quite unreasonable to expect the concept of citizenship to address the private domains of the family and the household. Nevertheless, insofar as women and men experience the "private" in different ways and have differential access to the "public" spheres of society, then traditional conceptions of citizenship will be inadequate, particularly in the era of globalization, given the social transformations it has led to.

Perhaps the most dramatic tendency of globalization in regards to gender is how it has differentiated women's work and created sharp new divisions. As Brigitte Young puts it: "The flexibilization of the labor market has produced greater equality between educated middle-class women and men while creating greater inequality among women" (Young 2000, 315). This growing social differentiation within women as a social category takes its sharpest form with migrant domestic workers servicing the needs of the Northern "mistress." The old South African distinction between "maids and madams" (see Cock 1980) that prevailed in the apartheid era is now reproduced worldwide. To put it bluntly, the Western professional woman needs a "wife" to take over her caring role, and this role is often filled by third-world women or, in the case of Western Europe, women from Eastern Europe. This accentuation of divisions between women has created new forms of social exclusion and also poses a challenge to the project of global feminism (see below).

One of the most interesting and fruitful ways to conceive of the new ways in which women are differentially integrated by globalization is through the concept of "global care chains." These are defined by Arlie Hochschild as "a series of personal links between people across the globe based on the paid or unpaid work of caring" (Hochschild 2001, 131). When a Mexican woman goes to work in a Los Angeles household, or an Eastern European woman comes to Paris or Berlin to work, she effectively becomes part of a global chain providing care services. She usually leaves behind a family and children and may have to "buy in" a local woman to take over her own household roles. As Hochschild puts it: "As mothering is passed down the race/class/nation hierarchy, each women becomes a provider and hires a wife" (Hochschild 2001, 137). It is globalization that has helped create a global flow of migrants (predominantly female) and a demand for service workers in the global cities and elsewhere in the global North.

Imperialism was described by Lenin as a chain linking the developed and developing world in a combined future. There is now much attention being paid to "global commodity chains" going, for example, from the Chilean grape grower to the metropolitan dinner table. We can broaden this concept into one that examines a global value chain that traces a commodity or service from conception to consumption (see Kaplinsky 2000). From there it is a necessary step to extend the concept of value to embrace not only production but also reproduction, where the care chain comes in to ensure the smooth reproduction of the world's workers. To the optimistic globalizer ideologist, these care chains are just a side effect (an "externality") of economic processes. From a critical transformationalist perspective, we note, however, not only the huge social impact this process has but also how it destroys traditional social relations while creating new ones that are no less inequitable. Certainly, present-day imperialism has created "commodification" of social relations on a worldwide scale.

In conclusion, we must stress that gender divisions are an integral and central element in the processes of social exclusion in the era of globalization. Both at the level of opportunity and of outcome, women are almost universally at a disadvantage. The Gender Empowerment Measure (GEM) was developed by the UNDP in 1995 to assess gender inequality in economic and political opportunities. The GEM takes into account such factors as female participation in politics and in professional and technical occupations, and the gap between female and male earnings. In 2002 it was found that there was enormous variation across the world, from less than 0.300 at one end of the spectrum to around 0.800 in relation to a maximum or equality level of nearly 1.000 for the Scandinavian countries. While poor countries on the whole earn low marks for women's empowerment, there are exceptions; the Bahamas and Trinidad score higher than Italy and Japan, for example (UNDP 2002, 23). This indicates that women's advancement is not guaranteed by the development of capitalism.

The other measure of gender inequality developed by the UNDP is the Gender-Related Development Index (GDI), which adjusts the Human Development Index (HDI) for inequalities in the *achievements* of women and men. If gender equality prevailed, the HDI and GDI would be the same. What we find, in fact, is that the GDI is lower everywhere without exception, although there are significant variations across countries. The GDI encapsulates a range of data from life expectancy, literacy rates, and educational enrollment rates to estimated earned income. As expected, the Scandinavian countries have high GDI levels, around 0.9 (of a maximum of 1.0); "medium" human development countries such as Mexico, the Russian Federation, and the Philippines score around 0.7; and "low" human development countries such as Pakistan, Nigeria, and Haiti score between 0.3 and 0.4. It is interesting and significant that some countries—such as Australia, Uruguay, Jamaica, Sri Lanka, Venezuela, and the Philippines—have a higher GDI than HDI. This indicates that gender policies can have a positive impact even when the HDI is not high.

THE FEMINIZATION OF POVERTY

If the 1980s were the decade of labor deregulation and "flexibilization" they were also, arguably, a period when a generalized feminization of labor activity took place. This entailed not only an increase in the proportion of women in the paid labor force but also the breaking down of exclusionary barriers to women's participation in hitherto "male" occupations. However, this increase in the level of social inclusion for women was not always advantageous. A study carried out between 1975 and 1995 of a sample of countries in the South found that in 75 percent of cases, female participation in the labor force had increased. However, this was nearly everywhere associated with the increased "flexibilization" of labor as demanded by the structural-adjustment programs. The World Bank was forced to admit in 1995 that "women [workers] are often more vulnerable than men, disproportionately concentrated in low-wage sector, or occupations and often segregated into the informal sector. Nor surprisingly, their relative position has often deteriorated during structural adjustment" (World Bank 1995, 171).

Thus we can see how the so-called feminization of (paid) work leads also to the feminization of poverty. A dramatic example of the gendered nature of work and poverty comes from the transition countries. Under the state socialist systems the proportion of women engaged in the formal economy was very high, and gender equality in employment was universally enshrined in law. With the unleashing of market forces in the 1990s this was to change, and women's "social duty" to work was largely discontinued. As the World Bank admits: "Women's employment choices may be constrained by increased labor market discrimination as evidenced by layoffs of women before men and open discrimination in job advertisements" (World Bank 1995, 72). Child care has become much more scarce and expensive, which inevitably acts as an exclusionary barrier for women seeking to (re)enter the labor market. The hardships and uncertainties of the transition to market rule also fall predominantly on women, given their continuing (and increasing) role in keeping the household functioning.

A broad review of women in the process of economic transformation (East and South) found that "whether per capita income has increased, stagnated or decreased, women have been over-represented among the losers or under-represented among the winners" (Aslanbegui, Pressman, and Summerfield 1994, 2). The gendered nature of economic transformation might take different forms depending on historical context and the particular political process, but it is invariably disadvantageous to women as a social category. So, for example, in the reunification of Germany it was the women workers of East Germany who were the real losers. Female participation rates were high there, and by the 1970s half the labor force was female. All this was to change after the reunification of Germany in the 1990s as women were driven back into the home, particularly women over thirty-five years of age. This patriarchal "solution" to the employment problems attendant on reunification was assisted, as one study shows, by the fact that "West German institutions and regulations concerning the labor market, the tax system, family allowances and female employment are still based on a conservative model that views a woman's place as primarily in the home" (Rudolph, Applebaum, and Maier 1994, 26).

The ideology of machismo was also prevalent, of course, in the authoritarian regimes of Latin America in the 1970s, and it carried through during the process of democratization in the 1990s. Women came to bear the main brunt of the social and economic policies of dictatorships such as that of Pinochet in Chile. As neo-liberalism disarticulated the preexisting social networks, women came to the fore to ensure the survival of their families. The whole household economy became geared to survival, and community networks, mobilized mainly by women, ensured basic necessities such as food. When democracy was reborn in the 1990s, gender issues could no longer be ignored or subsumed under a fascist ideology of gender roles. Women had gained considerable political resources in the struggles against the dictatorships, and now the gender agenda was to be "mainstreamed" by government. In practice what emerged was "neo-liberalism with a human face"; at best a more "gender-blind" approach to social development was taken, one that did not actively seek to discriminate against women.

What we must conclude is that the feminization of poverty cannot be approached simply from the perspective of low incomes. For example, the horrifying phenomenon of the world's "100 million missing women" (due to gender-specific pregnancy terminations and artificially low survival rates) cannot be explained simply in terms of economics. Low income in and of itself can explain very little about gender inequality. As Amartya Sen puts it, while analyzing the "missing women," a narrow income-inequality approach "has the effect of contributing to the neglect of other ways of seeing inequality and equity, which has far-reaching bearing on the making of economic policy" (Sen 2000, 107–8). Inequality comes in a multitude of guises much better captured by the concept of social exclusion than a purely economic emphasis on income. That gender inequality cannot be reduced to income differentials is what we learn from the "missing women," an extreme form of discrimination but one that is reproduced in many other ways across the world.

The global social-exclusion focus this book seeks to develop has had a central gender dimension from its inception. Arguably, this approach can enrich gender analysis, making it more multidimensional and taking it squarely into the policy domain. Clearly discrimination on the grounds of sex is a form of social exclusion. While poor women may suffer the main burden of these social exclusions, economically more secure women in the North may also suffer from gender discrimination. Despite the great diversity lying behind the category of women, there is a general gender dimension to social exclusion and to the uneven or unjust forms of social inclusion that are developed. The ILO has now accepted that "gender, as social exclusion, is a historical concept and stresses the need and possibility of change" (Ulshoefer 1998, 128). We must, then, bring to the fore the question of agency both in maintaining the structures of inequality and exclusion and in mounting challenges to these and developing a process of progressive social transformation.

From the 1980s onward, gender equality became a major concern of the international economic institutions and particularly the World Bank. It has now become an integral part of all development projects to carry out a gender-impact assessment; "gender-proofing" programs has become universally accepted (at least in principle). The mainstreaming of gender equality issues represented a major policy shift but not one without its critics who accuse the likes of the World Bank of simply coopting a feminist discourse. Macroeconomic policy is still firmly biased in favor of men, and the incorporation of women is due more to economic necessity that a concern with inclusion or equity. There is an assumption that discrimination is, in economic terms of resource utilization, irrational; therefore the rise of the market will necessarily favor equity and thus undermine prejudice and discrimination. Yet equating tradition with discrimination and modernity/market with equity is not borne out in practice.

The main weakness of the mainstream economic attempts at engendering policy are their unswerving focus on paid work and neglect of the reproductive economy, that is, the social sphere where gender relations are so central. The new household economics understands the importance of gender relations but reads these in purely economic terms by seeking an "optimal" distribution of resources within the family. In dealing only in monetary terms and focusing only on paid work, this perspective inevitably misses the main ways in which human development is a gendered process. "It ignores the human resource aggregates of the 'reproductive economy,' the indicators of population, health, nutrition, education, skills" (Elson 1994, 42). From the dominant economic perspective it is simply assumed that women are infinitely elastic as a resource and can be moved into the "productive economy" as required while maintaining their dominant role in the social reproduction of the household, their families, and their communities.

It is women's roles in sustaining their communities that is one of the main silences of the social-capital approach to human development today. While, at one level, it may be welcome to see the World Bank moving beyond an economic approach to engage with the social domain, from a gender perspective this move is not unproblematic. To build on preexisting social capital (essentially community networks of solidarity) may, in practice, mean building on a social structure that inherently discriminates against women. The whole communitarian agenda, underlying the conservative implementation of the social-capital agenda, is based squarely on a traditional conception of the sexual division of labor. When the World Bank endorses the existing family form as the key focus for the development of social capital, it inevitably tends to perpetuate and actively reproduce patriarchal structures, norms, and expectations. This is not to dismiss the concept of social capital altogether, but we do need to beware of the gender impact of seemingly innocent concepts.

Whatever its pitfalls and limitations, it still remains the case that many interesting policy developments have emerged in recent years to combat the social exclusion of women. For example, there are now more than forty countries that have adopted what are known as gender-sensitive budgets, a means whereby civil society can make governments accountable for their commitments to gender equality. They work through a gender-focused examination of national budgets to establish whether fiscal policy is encouraging gender equality or not. For the UNDP, the gender-responsive budgets "are a way of ensuring consistency between social commitments to achieve gender equality goals—such as in education or work—and the resources allocated" (UNDP 2002, 80). From the radical participatory budgeting experiment of Porto Alegre and other cities with progressive governments in Brazil, to Australia and the UK, or India and the Philippines there have been diverse local, regional, and national attempts to counter the feminization of poverty.

THE GLOBAL SEX TRADE

While trafficking in people is nothing new in human history, the era of globalization has seen a huge expansion and flourishing of this trade in legal, illegal, and semi-legal forms. It is estimated that around four million women are involved in the global sex trade every year. UNICEF does not have precise figures but believes that millions of children suffer from sexual exploitation worldwide. This global sex trade is clearly thriving, a genuine growth industry for the new global informational capitalism. Clearly it is facilitated by the spread of electronic communications, which has given impetus to a massive pornography industry, and it has also been made much more accessible (than even twenty years ago) through much cheaper travel to the worldwide locations that are the sites of the new global sex trade. A symptom of globalization it may be, but it is also, of course, a massive human rights crisis. Some of the most vulnerable members of society have become prey to ruthless "entrepreneurs" who buy and sell people, their organs, their senses, and their capacity to work, in conditions where they have little capacity for redress in law or through collective social organization and action.

The global sex trade is part and parcel of globalization, but it also reflects the prevailing sexist and racist ideologies in Western society. It is gendered (due to prevailing hetero-patriarchal notions, it is predominantly women's bodies that are used and abused) and it is racial (it is "exotic Oriental" and other non-Western women that are the main object of this industry), but it also nationalized (certain countries, such as Thailand, have become a focus for the global sex trade or particular aspects of it, such as child sex). It further represents the ultimate spread of an unregulated market and can readily be analyzed in terms of the supply and demand forces that create it.

It reflects the growing "commodification" of Western life, with the body being only another commodity to be bought and sold in the marketplace, and is now an integral element of life in many developing countries. It is also, of course, a form of social inclusion, insofar as these women and children are sucked into the maelstrom of globalization, albeit a perverse form of inclusion. It is now thought by some commentators that the global sex trade has replaced the arms and drugs trades as the most profitable line of business for the new flourishing global criminal networks (estimated income is US$52 billion a year), another symptom of the perverse nature of growth and social inclusion that globalization can generate.

The global sex trade takes many forms, ranging from the entertainment industry and tourist-related activities to bonded labor and slavery now being (re)produced by capitalism's most advanced expression: globalization. It is also related to patterns of migration and the flows of workers across national frontiers. As Peterson notes: "A now extensive literature reveals the increasing volume of sex work, its dependence on racial and heterosexist stereotypes, its relationship to labor markets and migration flows, and its costs in health and, especially, in vulnerable women's and children's lives" (Peterson 2003, 104). It is now widely recognized that there is a global trade in people for sex and other forms of work, that these workers are exploited, and that they suffer terrible privations, brutality, and even death. Rather than take that area for analysis, I have chosen to focus on the less visible end of the global "commodification" of the body.

A case study from the "more respectable" mail-order bride service industry may provide more insight into the global sex trade than an examination of the more underground forms of the sex trade. It illustrates well the "normalization" of trade in people and the complex interplay between "private" and "public" under late capitalism. A randomly accessed UK-based Internet marriage agency specializing in Thai women begins by explaining how today's technology allows the "discerning gentleman" to go beyond the traditional ordering arrangements of the past to access directly the women on offer. These are described as "respectable, decent, single, marriage minded Oriental ladies," although the epithet of "Thai babes" for the younger cohort on offer somewhat elides the distance it seeks to build in relation to the sex industry. A standard Internet FAQ (frequently asked questions) feature details the "do's and don'ts" in relation to "Thai culture." In particular, the "client" is warned that sex before marriage is taboo, and that the company takes its "in *loco parentis*" very seriously in relation to the women it is offering up for marriage to Westerners.

So, who might access this particular corner of the human-trafficking market? It is purportedly aimed at men who "are disillusioned with the kind of de-feminized, self-centred, mercenary minded lady, who is only out for what she can get." The male demand being assured, the service explains why there might be an offer of brides from Thailand: "There are many more women than men in Thailand, and a great shortage of eligible men." These men "often [have] more than one wife and several occasional girlfriends. Not good husband material." Western men are expected to be "loving, caring, faithful, and [to] provide the long term security they crave." In practice, they often submit their mail-order brides to virtual slavery and seem to assume that murder of their chattel is not a major criminal offense, as can be seen in some defense arguments when they come to court occasionally. It is hardly surprising that the International Anti-Slavery Society has made the trafficking of humans a major priority for its campaigns in the twenty-first century. It is quite clear that even the more "respectable" side of the global sex trade is in fact simply trading in human beings. As Peterson writes: "The market in brides has parallels with the prostitution industry insofar as heterosexist and racist desires constitute a pull factor and economic desperation constitutes a push factor that makes a market in women as sexual/domestic/caretaking/spousal service providers a lucrative business" (Peterson 2003, 109). People take seriously the message of neo-liberalism that the marketplace is open to all and that globalization provides great opportunities for those who will grasp them. Unfortunately, the reality is more often sordid and exploitative. For the mail-order bride, the best is a difficult situation trying to make the best of things, often to help out a family at home; at worst, her prospect is death.

The female body is also exploited in many other ways. Women are brought from the transition countries to Western Europe, from the Philippines to Nigeria and from East Asia to North America to become workers in the global sex industry. This is a segmented labor market like any other. While Thai women have moved into higher-paid segments of the market, the local market is provided with women from Burma, Laos, or Vietnam. The female body is made a commodity, and its geographical displacement has been extended and accelerated. As with the "nimble fingers" of the female workers in the 1970s mentioned above, there is a strong racist mythology that goes with the packaging of this commodity today. The new technologies allow for a dynamic presentation of the sexual commodity wrapped in all the imperialist images of the exotic "other," now made accessible for the "ordinary" Western man and not just the colonialist of old who raped as he plundered. The virtual economy forms an integral and facilitating part in the creation of a real global political economy of the body.

As Ursula Biemann notes, "Whether it is an offspring of military camps or a by-product of Western off-shore operations, women are displaced and drawn into the global economy through sexual labour" (Biemann 2002, 85). Imperialist bases in the developing world have been a key locus for the development of the global sex trade, which has now vastly expanded. The trade exists for the main in a "gray economy" that is not quite legal but is not usually pursued vigorously by the law. Receiving countries in Western Europe can claim that this trade is part of the entertainment industry and that the developing countries receive much-needed hard currency remittances. This trade also overlaps with the question of migration. It is precisely the border controls of the West, keen not to allow the same free mobility of labor that it claims for capital and finance, that drives much of the global sex trade into illegality. This can only reinforce the social exclusion of the workers involved insofar as they are deprived of all legal protection.

As to the sexual exploitation of children, Manuel Castells writes that "they have become sexual commodities in a large-scale industry, organized internationally through the use of advanced technology, and by taking advantage of the globalization of tourism and images" (Castells 1998, 154–55). In North America alone it was estimated in the mid-1990s that there were probably a quarter of a million child prostitutes. The second half of the 1990s saw a whole string of child sexual exploitation scandals across Western Europe. In Thailand, a center for Western paedophilia "tourists," there were estimated to be around three-quarters of a million child prostitutes in 2000.

Children as disposable sexual commodities are part of a long history of the abuse of children, but the trade's fluid, worldwide nature is something new. The market is now everywhere; it has invaded every nook and cranny of public and private space in society. Criminal networks readily connect up supply and demand when a given commodity—for example, child sex—is deemed illegal. The deregulation of almost every level of social life makes it easy to escape detection. There are fewer societal norms to control this trade, and the crisis of the family, although sometimes overstressed, can be seen as an inevitable result of the attack on the household by neo-liberal austerity policies. Legal reform, increased resources, and a heightened public awareness mean there are some moves to thwart this perverse symptom of globalization. Meanwhile, some one million children enter the multimillion dollar commercial sex trade every year.

For Biemann, those caught up in the global sex trade "are the embodiment of the abstract financial flows that feed the global economy" (Biemann 2002, 83). The global flows of money and bodies are equally emblematic of the global market order we live in, but while the first is invisible, the latter is corporeal. Both global flows also have their legal and illegal facets. The global sex trade is, in a sense, the "embodiment" of global money flows. Where the global political economy of the body differs from that of money is that human beings have become commodities. Racial and gender stereotypes are the basis on which the perverse inclusion of women in the global political economy of sex is carried out. Cynthia Enloe, early in the globalization debates, prompted us to examine how Asian women's sexuality could be packaged and traded across borders in a way that reproduced but also "modernized" colonial era representations of third-world women as a passive and exotic "other" (Enloe 1990). But sex tourism is only one part of the broader global economy of gender.

Women today represent the vast majority of refugees and migrant workers. Pushed and pulled by the pressures created by the changing international division of labor—as much as wars—women are on the move as never before. In this regard Jan Pettman is correct to point out that "a significant part of international labor migration is in the form of those going into domestic service" (Pettman 1996, 195). Up to two million Asian women domestic workers provide cheap domestic labor in the Middle East and Japan. This phenomenon, a clear symptom of globalization, also reinforces the national sexual division of labor. In the United States the Central American or Mexican maid was one of the fastest growing occupational categories in the 1980s (see Romero 2002). So, modernity reinforces, reproduces, and intensifies traditional forms of oppression and exploitation in relation to the political economy of gender. Finally, we see from this section that the global is highly personal (in its effects) and how (for many people) the personal is today inextricably bound up with the global in less than beneficial ways. A gendered understanding of globalization illuminates how this new order has sought to make commodities of all elements of life, including the most private and hitherto sacrosanct aspects of humanity such as human relationships, the rights of children, and people's dignity.

GLOBAL FEMINISM

Given the extent of global gender inequalities, what are the prospects for redressing the balance in favor of equity? From the perspective of liberal feminism, gender inequality is linked to legal parameters that do not recognize equal rights between the sexes. Prejudices are presented as an unfortunate hangover from less enlightened times or the prerogative of so-called backward societies. The policy response called for focuses, logically enough, on education and legal reform. Thus multilateral economic organizations such as the World Bank make education for girls and women a priority. The United Nations symbolically enshrined the principles of gender equality in the 1945 Charter and has since then, through the 1995 Beijing Summit and beyond, recognized the global nature of gender inequality and its pervasiveness across cultural and social systems. A gender-equality discourse is now central to the ongoing moves to achieve some form of stable governance for the processes of economic globalization under market rule.

Liberal feminism has certainly had a remarkable achievement in successfully mainstreaming gender concerns in the development and democracy policymaking circles. However, we can question whether this success is at the cost of political clarity and a radical pursuit of gender equality worldwide. In the first place we may legitimately ask, along with Christine Chinkin, "whether legal prescription, and in particular international legal prescription, can generate fundamental societal change" (Chinkin 1999, 95). In practice there is a huge disparity between what the law lays down in terms of equal rights and what happens on the ground. Nor can the power of the law operate with equal effectiveness in all societies. The second problem with the liberal legal framework of gender equality is that it usually works on the basis that men are the norm. It may work effectively where women play similar roles to men, as in Western public employment, but not so well where gender differences are more pronounced and recognition of that difference might make more sense than stressing a spurious equality.

There are other strands in Western feminism that have carried out more radical critiques than these of liberal feminism. Radical feminism has focused on the overarching patriarchal nature of all societies that created structural male domination of society not amenable to simple legal reform. Rather than seeking equality with men, radical feminism has stressed the "difference" of women and might ultimately advocate a form of separation as the appropriate strategy for women. Socialist feminism developed a materialist standpoint on gender oppression in terms of the needs of the capitalist system. The struggle for women's rights was usually seen as part and parcel of the broader struggle for working-class advancement. This could sometimes lead to a critical attitude toward mainstream feminism, seen as "divisive" by some socialists. There was also a strong critique of the "bourgeois feminism" that focused on changing the law rather than the underlying social structures of oppression. Today, many of these divides have been superseded, in part by the new order of globalization that has set new parameters for creating the conditions for gender equality.

From a global gender perspective there is the overarching problem that all Western feminisms are inevitably particular to the part of the world that has generated the discourses and practices. Thus we find the popular anthologies edited by Robin Morgan, *Sisterhood Is Powerful* (1970) and even its sequel *Sisterhood Is Global* (1984) operating within a very Western and white perspective, on the whole. These books presented feminism as a concern of Western middle-class white women, excluding or marginalizing women of color in the North and being almost totally oblivious to third-world women. When third-world women did become a focus of concern, it was in a manner that tended to unify and homogenize women in a victim mode rather than seeing the women in various parts of the Third World as actors and activists. The "women in development" school of the 1980s did, however, begin to overcome these weaknesses and place the women of the majority world within the broader context of colonialism and imperialism as well as gender forms of oppression.

In Western feminism itself, black feminists in the 1980s also worked to disrupt the homogeneous front presented by earlier feminisms. In speaking for the whole category of women, white Western women were being ethnocentric. In not recognizing the centrality of racism and colonialism in shaping most women's lives Western feminism elided a central feature of oppression. Thus the notion of a universal sisterhood can be seen as a liberal myth. We need to deconstruct the notion of woman and recognize that there is a hierarchy of oppression (although this notion could itself be seen as divisive). This wave of feminist critique showed that social exclusion reflected race as well as gender. In the postcolonial critique of Western feminism (see Mohanty 1992) there was a further inclusion of non-Western women that effected a significant cultural broadening of international feminism in ways that are still having their effects today at international women's forums.

The notion of global feminism—once deconstructed by black and developing-world feminists—can play a powerful mobilizing role in the era of globalization. It has generated, through a set of interlinked transnational, national, and local social movements, a new global solidarity that confronts neo-liberal globalization ethically as well as politically. Women's internationalism has effectively redefined the meaning of international solidarity and begun to articulate a new politics of transformation adequate to the globalized, informationalized capitalism under which we live. Thus a conference on reproductive technology held in Dhaka in 1989 argued that "patriarchal, industrial, commercial and racist domination over life" was a global issue for all women, regardless of class and ethnicity, and that it demanded a global response: "We appeal to all women and men to unite globally against dehumanizing technologies and express our solidarity with all those who seek to uphold and preserve the diversity of life on our planet and the integrity and dignity of all women" (cited in Waterman 1998, 181).

We may well question whether global feminism exists in any real sense, given the social and political distance between, for example, Western "identity politics" and poor women in developing countries. We can certainly question Castells's optimistic proclamation about "the end of patriarchy" (Castells 1996, chap. 4). However, there is no doubt that women's internationalism has established a clear "best practice" in the arena of contestation to globalization. These movements have innovatively deployed the new technologies of information capitalism to inform, mobilize, and shift the terms of cultural debate. Women's movements from the early 1970s onward have developed networked forms of organization that can be seen as precursors of the current anti-globalization movement practices. Finally, the international women's movement has taken the lead in building bridges to other social movement, such as the peace and ecology movements and also the international trade union movement, which went through a genuine "engendering" process in the 1990s.

Global feminism has also placed the issue of citizenship's fundamentally gendered nature firmly on the political agenda. From its classical origins to its modern form, citizenship has been modeled on the male citizen; women have not only been excluded but constructed in opposition. Thus the public domain was seen as male and the (inferior) private domain as female. The state granted to men rights of property and of suffrage while denying these to women until recently (if a long historical view is taken). The domestic labor of women that ensures social reproduction was devalued while the norm was set by paid formal employment in the public arena. Even radical theories of citizenship have taken for granted the public/ private divide, either not seeing its gender implications or arguing that questioning it would dissolve the very notion of citizenship. Yet, as Ruth Lister notes, "the dichotomization of public and private serves to rule out of political bounds those impediments to women's citizenship which are located in the private sphere" (Lister 1997, 125).

For social exclusion on the basis of gender to be overcome, a properly gendered political theory of transformation needs to be developed. A merely formal "equal" citizenship in the public domain may mask patriarchal dominance in the private domain. Violence against women and women's control of their own fertility are issues of strategic gender interest that cannot be legislated in a gender-neutral manner. While global feminism has gained great strength from the acceptance of women's rights as universal human rights, it has certain limits as a strategy. Certainly it has engaged with the issue of global governance and has mainstreamed gender at that level. However, the world is not global in a homogeneous way and, as Isin and Wood argue, "removing the battle for women's rights from the local context can sever its apparent connections to economic structures and democratic processes that have a chance of success in the state" (Isin and Wood 1999, 78). In short, global feminism still needs to develop and articulate a combined local, national, and regional strategy. Women's movements are no less prone to routine, bureaucracy, and cooptation than men's movements. But we must always bear in mind what Peterson calls "the singularly most transformative feminist insight," namely, that the "privileging of masculinity—*not necessarily men*—is key to naturalizing the . . . power relations that constitute structural hierarchies" (Peterson 2003, 14). Patriarchy's denigration of the feminine is an integral element in global capitalism's continued and reinforced subordination of poor countries and poor people generally, which are devalorized by the managers and beneficiaries of neo-liberal globalization.

CONCLUSION

This chapter has examined the interrelations between gender and global inequality. As the World Commission on the Social Dimension of Globalization concluded: "There is a growing body of evidence illustrating the ways in which substantial numbers of women have been adversely affected by globalization, both absolutely as well as in relation to men" (World Commission on the Social Dimension of Globalization 2003, no. 215, p. 61). Professional women who have benefited from globalization are far outweighed by farming women and those in micro and small enterprises that have been deleteriously affected by free-market economics. The example of the global sex trade illustrates well an earlier point, namely, that integration into the world economy is no panacea to overcome social exclusion. The perverse or malign integration of women into the global commodity chain of sex is not a progressive answer to the lack of social opportunities in developing countries in the South or in the transitional economies of the East. As Peterson puts it, we are moving toward a world in which "infants, human organs, sexualized bodies, intimate caring, sensual pleasures, and spiritual salvation are all for sale" (Peterson 2003, 78).

In conclusion, we asked what global feminism, in all its multiple facets, contributes to the making of a transformative politics taking us beyond social exclusion. Gender is at the heart of the social division of labor (the gender division of labor), but it also operates at the cultural level, producing discrimination, marginalization, and the social exclusion of women. Thus a transformative politics of gender must, necessarily, take up the political economy of gender disadvantage though redistribution of resources, but it must also recognize difference rather than subsume women under generic equality concerns. As Nancy Fraser sums up this debate: "Insofar as women suffer at least two analytically distinct kinds of injustice, they necessarily require at least two analytically distinct kinds of remedy—both redistribution and recognition" (Fraser 1995, 79). While in the real world this distinction might seem somewhat fuzzy, it is an analytical distinction we should always keep in mind as we move on to consider social exclusion in terms of race (Chapter 6) and of class (Chapter 7) before moving (back) to develop a transformative vision of life beyond social exclusion (Chapter 8).

6

Race, Migration, and Citizenship

Debates on racial and ethnic inequality often end up in fierce polemics over the precise meanings of the terms. The term *race* certainly is often deployed as an ideological construct and can in itself be oppressive. It could arguably be seen as part of a broader category of ethnic divisions, but this terminology is also subject to considerable debate. We will simply take *race* to mean a social division in society based on color (itself a social and political category, of course), whether self-defined or imposed by others. Along with the great upsurge of international migration in the era of globalization, race has been a major marker of social exclusion. It has also, however, generated one of the most fruitful debates on citizenship, along the lines of multi-culturalism or cosmopolitanism, which provides new avenues for social transformation beyond simply calling for social inclusion as a counter to social exclusion.

This chapter also explores the hypothesis that we are entering an era of global apartheid where ethnic and other divisions become entrenched and the basis for societal organization as apartheid did in South Africa before the free elections of 1994 led to the victory of the nonracial African National Congress. More than just an analogy, this metaphor seeks to capture the deeply divisive and regressive nature of an unbridled globalization that does not have an equality and diversity agenda at its core. Amy Chua has argued provocatively that: "The global spread of free market democracy has ... been a principal, aggravating cause of ethnic instability and violence throughout the non-Western world" (Chua 2003, 187). This argument flies in the face of complacent neo-liberal myths that the free market is race blind (as it was gender blind), and it also undermines claims for the universal applicability and even desirability of Western (read: United States) versions of democracy.

THE COLOR OF POVERTY

As Loic Wacquant notes: "The colour line of which the black ghetto is the most visible institutional expression is so ingrained in the makeup of the American urban landscape that it has become part of the order of things: racial division is a thoroughly taken for granted constituent of the organization of the metropolitan economy society and polity" (Wacquant 1993, 373–74). While the Civil Rights reform of the mid-1960s had buried the legal racism encapsulated in the Jim Crow system, the century that had elapsed since the Civil War had allowed for an entrenched racial system to replace slavery as a means of oppression and exploitation. While there is an important ongoing debate on the relative importance of race and class in determining social inequality and exclusion in the United States (see Massey and Denton 1993, 84–88), the continuous disadvantages suffered by African Americans are evident enough, as is the primacy of race in explaining segregation.

It is the spatial concentration of black poverty in the United States that is its most notable characteristic. As Massey and Denton put it: "Geographically concentrated poverty is built into the experience of urban blacks by racial segregation" (Massey and Denton 1993, 118). It is the interaction between that social group's poverty and social exclusion levels, and its residential segregation that set up a dynamic of concentrated deprivation and disadvantage. Thus in Chicago's poorer West-side and South-side neighborhoods, 90 percent of the population was black as social polarization increased from the 1970s onward (Morenoff and Tienda 1997, 68). Since the days of the Great Society in the 1960s these areas have been in steady decline as Federal funds for urban community development steadily have declined, welfare and unemployment payments have increased, and the decline of health facilities has been matched only by the increase in crime rates.

In the early 1960s, prior to the big Civil Rights victories, one of the main manifestations of institutional racism in the United States was an unemployment rate for black men and women nearly double that of their white counterparts. In 2002 the official unemployment rate for black men and women was *more* than twice that of their white counterparts (Magdoff et al. 2003, 2). Given that blacks had made gains during the low unemployment rate period of the 1990s, a 10 percent unemployment rate for black males was a sharp reminder that institutional racism still prevailed. Unemployment rates are invariably a crucial indicator for social exclusion, whether on racial, ethnic, or religious grounds. Thus one of the main issues underlying the rise of a Civil Rights movement in Northern Ireland in the late 1960s was an unemployment rate for Catholics that was at least twice that for Protestants, a differential that persisted for decades in spite of many fair-employment laws and official pronouncements.

A focus on income alone would allow us to argue that African Americans are much better off in global terms than the poor in India and China, for example. However, if we take a basic indicator of well-being such as life expectancy, we find that African Americans are not only suffering the *relative* deprivation of lower incomes vis-à-vis US whites, but also the *absolute* deprivation of lower life expectancy compared to poor people in India and China, two of the poorest countries in the world. The causal influences on the contrast between income inequality and that of survival include following Amartya Sen's path-breaking "capability deprivation" model of poverty: "social arrangements and community relations such as medical coverage, public health care, school education, law and order, prevalence of violence and so on" (Sen 1999, 22–23). In other words, it is not just poverty that is "colored" but the whole social structure and the mechanisms of social policy that result in social exclusion.

Apart from the US apartheid system, the system of South Africa stands out as a form of institutionalized racism and social exclusion. As Gary Marx puts it: "White supremacy was the glue that held South Africa together, inscribed in the very foundation of a polity born of historical conflict and exclusion" (Marx 1998, 119). The racial order in South Africa was not a simple result of biological distinctions, as is seen in the varying legal treatment of the so-called colored population according to political needs. While apartheid built on prior racial prejudices of the English-speaking and Afrikaaner whites, these do not in themselves explain the institutional outcome. As Steve Biko once wrote, racial domination "was not a mistake on the part of whites, but a deliberate act." It served strategic economic and political interests, it helped forge a unitary nation-state based on racial social exclusion, and it consolidated state control by the minority white population.

When South African apartheid began to unravel in the early 1990s, it was largely because it had served its purpose, but it was also because of an effective challenge by the ANC's social inclusionary drive. However, the post-1994 democratic nonracial governments could hardly unravel the legacy of apartheid overnight. Poverty and unemployment in today's South Africa is still predominantly black in spite of the rise of a new black middle class. Nor could democratic inclusion undo the history of racial and ethnic divisions. While the ANC may have provided a unifying discourse against apartheid, it was less clear that it could now unify such a divided and polarized society. Nationalisms had, in the past, been constructed through a process of ethnic antagonism. This was still to be the case with the Zulu speakers of Kwazulu Natal, and it also seemed to underlie a new generalized antagonism toward migrant workers coming from bordering countries such as Mozambique.

That the color of poverty is not reducible to black-white divisions is clear also in the growing tensions and discriminatory practices in the Afro-Arab borderlands of North Africa. While the Arab conquest of North Africa goes back to the eighth century, the cultural denationalization of the Berbers in Morocco, Africa, Tunisia, and Lybia has modern roots. Arabization has led to a very real process of marginalization and social exclusion for African ethnic groups. The Arab/African conflict is probably sharpest today in the Sudan. Here Arabization and Islamization have been carried out, according to Francis Deny, "in a context of a racially stratified society that deemed the Arab people and their culture superior and the African blacks and their belief systems inferior" (cited in Prah 2001, 4). Arab race and traditions were deemed culturally superior, and discrimination against non-Arabs and non-Muslims reinforced segregation in this society.

In Sudan, as is often the case, ethnic divisions are overlaid by regional development patterns with the more "African" South suffering from extreme underdevelopment. This regional division of labor is based on a racial division of labor in which Africans are scarce among the mercantile-banking and state-sector strata and prevalent in the manual and informal sectors of the economy. Showing the heavy legacy of colonialism in creating this system based on divisions and discrimination, in Northern Sudan it is considered insulting to use the word *black*, which is associated directly with slavery. So strong is the perception that Northern, more Arabic Sudan is superior that, as nationalist leader Joseph Uduho explains, "in every passport given to any Sudanese, whether he be brown, semi-white, pitch-black, it is always said 'brown' in the colour. . . . It is one of those things" (cited in Prah 2001, 7). The color of oppression and exclusion is complex and cannot be reduced to a white-black divide.

Compared to US or South African racial divisions, Brazil has been portrayed as a paragon of racial democracy. While the state deployed a cultural language of color, it rejected racial categories and boundaries as a basis for segregation. Yet Brazil possesses a rigid social hierarchy and is one of the most unequal societies in the world. There is little doubt that those at the top of this society are universally white, and that lower down the pyramid society is much "darker." Afro-Brazilians are much more likely to be unemployed or in poorly paid jobs than their white counterparts, they have a shorter life expectancy, and they tend to live in distinct neighborhoods. While it is said that "money whitens" in Brazil, it is particularly difficult for blacks to break into the rigid hierarchical social system that characterizes Brazilian capitalism.

As Brazilian democracy deepened in the 1990s, the debate on the color of poverty came to the fore. Black identity began to emerge, and progressive political parties and the trade unions condemned racial discrimination explicitly. The state adapted a multi-cultural language directed at the Afro-Americans and also the surviving indigenous peoples of the Amazon. Yet the Workers' Party's most prominent black member, Benedicta da Silva (now a leading member in the Lula government), could still declare that "there is no color to socialism." Racial and ethnic distinctions were seen by many as divisive in the struggle for democracy and progressive social transformation. The myth of racial democracy has been enduring and has served as an obstacle to the formation of strong ethnic identities. Racism is a fact of life in Brazil, but it has been defined more in class terms. Nevertheless, the consolidation of democracy and the achievement of social inclusion in Brazil today certainly require a more explicit and direct confrontation with the color of poverty.

It is now necessary for us to broaden the picture to consider the understated role of ethnic divisions in the making of contemporary globalization and in the construction of democracy. For Chua, the neo-liberal promoters of globalization have sorely neglected the question of race and ethnicity because it is so explosive and because these divisions undermine the optimistic scenarios of the globalizers. If we look around the world, we see, according to Chua, "*market-dominant minorities*: ethnic minorities who, for widely varying reasons, tend under market conditions to dominate economically, often to a startling degree, the 'indigenous' majorities around them" (Chua 2003, 6). Thus the Chinese minority in Burma represents 5 percent of the population but owns 70 percent of the wealth. Elsewhere white minorities or some other ethnic groupings develop similar near monopolistic control over national wealth. It is clear there can be no "pure" economic class divisions separate from the divides of race and ethnicity. For Chua, it is precisely "the spread of global markets [that has] produced vast, inflammable ethnic wealth imbalances all over the world" (Chua 2003, 123). Preexisting disparities of wealth and power tend to be exacerbated by the opening up of free markets, as the absence of social control or regulation in the Polanyi sense can only deepen and harden existing divisions. There is here a deep source of division that questions the sustainability of the present mode of globalization in and of itself. Translated, or "scaled up" to the global level, this line of enquiry has obvious implications for the leading capitalist power (the United States), which is perceived globally as a "market dominant ethnic minority" a "white" citadel in the vast plains of the nonwhite non-Western majorities. The "great Satan" can thus easily be read in ethnic rather than religious terms.

PEOPLE ON THE MOVE

If race is a key marker of social exclusion at a national level, it is also a key facet in the rise of international migration and other forms of "people on the move" in the era of globalization. If a nation-state has been formed on the basis of a myth of racial or ethnic "purity," then mass immigration of "different" people is bound to destabilize it. Racism may be called ethno-centrism or, more politely, a distrust of foreigners, but however labeled it is discriminatory and corrosive of democracy. With migration we see most clearly how racism need not be based only on supposedly biological differences but may take cultural, religious, or linguistic forms of expressing difference with the "other." Cultural symbolic markers as much as phenotypic markers are mobilized by anti-Muslim racisms in Europe, similar to how language differences may be used to mark out the distance between Hispanics and Anglo-Americans in the United States, for example.

International migration must also be seen as an effect of the global inequalities between the developed North and the underdeveloped South. In the classical era of imperialism (1870–1914), as capitalism expanded on a world scale, it required an ever-increasing number of workers to open up these new areas. There was a mass

European migration to the Americas and Australasia. Other workers were absorbed into the manufacturing plants created by the Industrial Revolution, as with the continuous flow of Irish workers to Britain. In the post–Second World War period this influx of workers from less developed regions to work in the factories and service industries of the North continued. In the post–Cold War period migration from the collapsing Eastern economies increased. Overall, in the era of globalization the "push and pull" of migration is determined by the overarching socio-economic inequalities between the global North and the global South as workers seek out better conditions, usually at great personal risk and cost.

On a purely quantitative measure, international migration today is not as significant as it was in the era of imperialism. It has been estimated that at the turn of this century only 1.5 percent of the global labor force worked outside their country of origin (Cohen and Kennedy 2000, 202), and at least half of these were concentrated in sub-Saharan Africa and in the Middle East. In the European Union, which was supposed to usher in the free movement of labor as well as capital, less than 2 percent of the citizens worked across national frontiers in the mid-1990s, the same percentage as twenty years previously. Nevertheless, while migration flows may be less intense than during the classical imperialist period, they are more extensive insofar as globalization has tended to create an integrated world system. Castles and Miller argue in this regard that "international migration has never been as pervasive, nor as socioeconomically and politically significant, as it is today. . . . Never before has international migration seemed so pertinent to national security and so connected to conflict and disorder on a global scale" (Castles and Miller 1993, 260).

It is clear that the vast bulk of migration today still occurs within countries, usually from rural to urban areas, so why should international migration be seen as such an important facet of globalization? International migrants are a relatively small proportion of the world's workers (although 80 to 90 million workers is not a negligible social group), but they constitute a vital social link among different sectors of the global economy. They are also quite visible socially, being usually concentrated in certain cities or regions. As Cohen and Kennedy put it, "In political and sociological terms their movements are highly sensitive" (Cohen and Kennedy 2000, 202). This shifting population appears to be a sign of social transformations to come, as the world becomes more fluid and its inhabitants more mobile. However, social identities are likely to become more complex and fluid, we could argue, insofar as social differences between the local-born population and the migrant population mark out a terrain where the very future of democracy is at stake.

In assessing the social and political impact of international migration today we can start with what might be called elite migration. It is estimated that the largest proportion of migrants (up to 25 million) comprises employees of the transnational corporations that are the motor of globalization (see Chapter 2). Managers, consultants, information specialists, accountants, and engineers are skilled and highly paid migrant workers who find few impediments to international movement. They probably constitute the majority of workers leaving Western countries to work abroad for a period of time or semi-permanently. The top business elite is becoming a genuine transnational capitalist class (see Chapter 7) with a significant degree of geographical mobility. This group could be seen as the real exemplars of globalization, at home anywhere in the world insofar as they can stay in the same Hilton Hotel, and eat the same breakfast, read the same English-language newspaper, and watch the same CNN news as they would at home.

This elite transient population is overwhelmingly white; it is also primarily male. But women are now a much larger proportion of migrant workers as a whole than in the past, with some arguing that they now constitute the majority of international migrants. The global sex trade and the mail-order bride industry (see Chapter 5) are but one part of a new expanding global service economy where women predominate. We see regular press items claiming that European health services are dependent on Filipina nurses, for example. A cursory acquaintance with Western cities reveals that its hotel receptionists, waitresses, and cleaners come from third-world countries. The vast hidden sector of domestic service in the West—cooking, cleaning, ironing, *au pairing*—in the West is now work carried out predominantly by third-world women or, more recently, women from the transition economies of the East.

At the other end of the spectrum of international migration from the elite business class executives are the illegals, the asylum seekers, and the refugees. There is great fluidity to the category of undocumented workers who are sometimes illegal but tolerated or even encouraged, as with Mexican workers in the United States or North African workers in the European Mediterranean countries. There are also the notorious people smugglers, who have made a profitable business out of the trafficking of people across national frontiers. The vast majority of unskilled migrant workers come in under contracts that exploit them and undercut local labor. For example, until the system was disrupted by the First Gulf War, there were hundreds of thousands of Pakistani, Indian, and Thai workers employed in the Gulf States. Not surprisingly, these states "were worried about their increased dependence on foreign labor, which in a number of cases outnumbered the total citizens" (Cohen and Kennedy 2000, 209).

Today there are probably twenty million refugees (and asylum seekers) worldwide who seek a place of refuge from war or repression in their home country. Civil wars in sub-Saharan Africa, the Balkans, and elsewhere have generated a process of displacement that is unprecedented, at least since the Second World War. The United Nations High Commissioner for Refugees (UNHCR) recognizes the vastness and complexity of this process of social exclusion from one's native land. The category could also be extended to cover the internally displaced persons who are forced to leave their homes due to war or ecological disasters. Many states have erected complex and controversial procedures to assess which asylum seekers are fleeing persecution and which are deemed to be economic migrants. Certainly this is the most politicized area of international migration, with "good" refugees (say from communist countries) distinguished from what the popular press calls "bogus" asylum seekers.

Migration can also change the "color" of cities socially and politically in the rapidly evolving world of globalization. In the United States, the poorest city is Miami, where, not coincidentally, over 60 percent of the population are immigrants. What is interesting is that this mainly Spanish-speaking population is no longer composed solely (or even mainly) of right-wing Cubans fleeing Fidel Castro's regime. After the collapse of Argentina's economy in 2002, 175,000 Argentineans went straight to Miami in search of work; when Mexico joined NAFTA (North American Free Trade Association), a considerable number of the laid-off *maquiladoras* (makeup plant workers) ended up in Miami. Thus, Miami reflects the changing fortunes of Latin America within the borders of the United States and is an indication of how interlinked the new global world is in not only economic but also social and cultural terms.

We need to move beyond the conventional categories of the economic, political, and cultural dimension of globalization to add the critical yet under-researched ethnic dimension. This is what Arjun

Appadurai aptly calls an "ethnoscape," which he defines as "the landscape of persons who constitute the shifting world in which we live: tourists, immigrants, refugees, exiles, guest workers and other moving groups and persons [that] constitute the essential features of the world, and appear to affect the politics of and between nations to an unprecedented degree" (Appadurai 1990, 297). Certainly these people on the move are a minority in terms of the global population, but they have a marked social and cultural effect, because people do not move just as workers but take their whole culture with them. In the diasporas (for example, the overseas Chinese) and in the multicultural global cities the social and cultural impact of globalization is now becoming apparent. There are hybrid cultural forms now emerging that are demanding a new conception of citizenship.

The other side of international migration, however, is the increasing move toward tightening border controls. The notion of Fortress Europe is an example of this scenario. It envisages a land of opportunity and democracy for its citizens, one that will repel all "invaders" from the "badlands" lying beyond. In the newly unified Germany of the 1990s there was a sharp increase in racism as Turkish workers, for example, were blamed for unemployment in the East. Where immigration is tacitly allowed but not legally recognized, as in Japan, this leads to an acute social marginalization of the immigrant community. Overall, then, international migration has highlighted the porous nature of national boundaries and has also led to an increase in social exclusion. Except for a transnational business elite, most migrant workers are excluded from the mainstream of society, marginalized in low-paying, insecure work, and deprived of almost all political rights.

The issue of migration calls into question the internal consistency of the neo-liberal program, demanding as it does the free mobility of the factors of production, except for labor. The debates over migration, and even more, those around asylum seekers and refugees, bring to the fore the fraught future of actually existing globalization. The world is becoming more integrated in all ways and pressure is building up for labor to be mobile. Yet nation-states increasingly succumb to or actually promote racist "moral panics" in relation to those mobile workers. Laws are passed tightening border controls, and the inevitable corollary is an increase in illegal trafficking of workers. This leads to worsening conditions for workers, when it does not lead directly to their death en route or in horrific accidents caused by the lack of strong labor regulations. Immigration flows are embedded in the broader development of globalization, and pressure is building for some kind of reappraisal of traditional nationalist-chauvinist responses. As Saskia Sassen argues: "The changes brought about by the growing interdependencies in the world will sooner or later force a radical re-thinking of how we handle immigration" (Sassen 2002).

GLOBAL APARTHEID

One possibly fruitful way to conceptualize the new world order being created by globalization and social exclusion is by analogy with apartheid South Africa. In an admittedly polemical vein, educationalist Titus Alexander argues that "across a wide range of socio-economic indicators, there is a strong evidence for a profound parallel between South Africa and the world" (Alexander 1996, 13). If we take all the various socio-economic indicators, such as the Human Development Index, we find that the gap between the "developed" and the "developing" world is indeed similar to that between black and white South Africa in the era of apartheid. Whether it is life expectancy or infant mortality, literacy rates or health facilities, there is a qualitative as well as quantitative gap between the global North and the South every bit as structurally set as that between Africans and the descendants of white settlers in South Africa.

The parallels between South Africa and today's globalizing world economy go further, however. Apartheid's elaborate system of racial classification finds its contemporary counterpart (albeit far less totalizing) in byzantine Western nationality laws and procedures for classifying immigrants and asylum seekers and refugees (Alexander 1996, 14). Classification is crucial for control, and the intricacies and inconsistencies of South Africa's classifications of its "colored" population are not totally dissimilar to the World Bank's criteria when it seeks to classify "developing," "less developed," "least developed," or "underdeveloped" countries. In terms of their ideological justifications the apartheid regime and the new world order share a faith in Western, Christian, basically white values. There is even the same misuse of language, as when blacks were removed from the electoral register under the Representation of Blacks Act in South Africa and the United States waged a war of conquest on Iraq under the banner of a war of "liberation" for "democracy." Discourses all have their genealogies, and neo-liberal globalization finds its heritage in the now discredited apartheid ideology of racist South Africa.

Apartheid and the new global order also have an exclusionary dynamic at their core. The laws of apartheid were based explicitly on a principle of exclusion, justified by the principle of white superiority. Africans were excluded from the land, employment, the political process, and certain areas of the territory. Citizenship was a right exclusively for whites. The exclusionary model of nation-building can, however, be generalized far beyond the very particular case of apartheid South Africa. As Castles and Miller note: "Countries in which the dominant definition of the nation is that of a community of birth and descent . . . are unwilling to accept immigrants and their children as members of the nation" (Castles and Miller 1993, 223). This gives rise to exclusionary immigration policies and restrictive nationalization rules. Race and ethnicity are at the core of most Western conceptions of nation to such an extent that apartheid (any more than fascism) cannot really be seen simply as an unfortunate and bizarre aberration from the civilized norm. Rather, apartheid is as much part of the Western heritage as is the Enlightenment, at least from a majority-world viewpoint or perspective.

We have already seen above the extent to which race and ethnicity are major factors determining social exclusion within nations and when people cross national frontiers. In terms of developing the concept of global apartheid as an acute form of social exclusion, we should now consider the position of indigenous people in terms of global social exclusion and structural racism. As Rodolfo Stavenhagen—a special UN rapporteur on indigenous human rights—notes: "Indigenous peoples were never recognised as full-fledged members of society, usually remaining as wards of the state, after their lands and territories had been taken, their environment devastated, their cultures mutilated and their livelihoods destroyed by agents of empire, missionaries of God, government bureaucrats and corporate officers" (Stavenhagen 1999, 12). This picture prevailed in the Americas and Australasia, but it could also be extended to subordinated peoples across the world who have suffered this brutal form of social exclusion. Thus Australia's Aborigines and India's Untouchables share a world of social exclusion marked by cultural rejection and political powerlessness (Mendelsohn and Baxi 1994). The recent report of the World Commission on the Social Dimension of Globalization noted in this regard that "a particularly vulnerable group is indigenous peoples. Where their integration into the world economy has occurred . . . without adequate protection of their rights, livelihoods, and culture, they have suffered severely. In such cases investments in extractive industries, mega-hydroelectric dams, and plantations have led to massive dislocations, disruptions of live-lihoods, ecological degradation, and violation of basic human rights" (World Commission on the Social Dimension of Globalization 2003, no. 211, 46).

The poverty and marginalization of indigenous peoples can thus be seen to be not just a historical issue but a matter of immediate global concern. Their economic exploitation continues; denial of their full citizenship rights is also common. Before globalization came along with "global culture" seeking to remake the whole world in its image, the indigenous peoples had already been subject to a Western drive to assimilate. Indigenous peoples were simply not considered part of the nation, and that historical legacy cannot be overcome by pious modern-day commitments to multi-culturalism. The accumu-lated effect of the various forms of social exclusion inflicted on in-digenous peoples cannot be undone simply by inclusionary social policies.

The situation of indigenous peoples under the aegis of globaliza-tion highlights the shift in the way racism operates at a global level. For a whole historical period racism was linked to colonialism, but the end of colonialism did not mean that racism ceased to operate at the international level. Today racism arguably takes as one of its main forms "social exclusion," which is manifested in the system we have called global apartheid. The rights of minorities and indig-enous peoples are recognized in international law, but they continue to be subjected to oppression and exploitation. In 1965 there was an International Convention on the Elimination of all Forms of Racial Discrimination. Yet in 2001 the Third World Conference against Racism, Racial Discrimination, Xenophobia, and Related Intoler-ance, held in Durban, was dedicated to examining the scant progress made in the fight against racism and the struggle for universal citi-zenship. Colonialism is gone and so is apartheid, but race and ethnicity are still potent markers of disadvantage and discrimination. Indeed, following the end of the Cold War there has been a recrudescence of demonization of ethnic minority and immigrant groups in much of the West. Ali Mazrui develops the notion of global apartheid in this regard referring to increased incidents of overt racism across the North based on a "pan-Caucasianism" and the emergence of a new phase of global racism (Mazrui 1994).

We can now take a broader perspective on global apartheid as a way of conceptualizing the world of globalization that developed from the collapse of the Berlin Wall to the collapse of the Twin Towers. For the hyper-hegemonic Western power, the United States, the role that international communism once served as the "other" has now been replaced by international terrorism. The United States was redefined culturally as the homeland, and the rest of the world (apart from the coalition of the willing client-states) as "badlands," where alien and threatening, but ultimately inferior, species exist. It is as though there has been a return to the frontier mentality, when countries like the United States or Argentina were built through the extermination of their indigenous peoples. The world is one, according to the globalizers, but it is a very divided world and one that is becoming ever more polarized not only in economic terms but also in strategic and geo-cultural terms.

Behind the word *terrorism*, of course, lurks *Islamicism* in the Western political imaginary. There is a clear case for applying the paradigm of globalization and social exclusion to the "Islamic question" rather than the crude and debasing language of terrorism. Against conceptions of Islam as part of some battle of civilizations a la Huntingdon or a primordial response motivated by irrational religious impulses, Olivier Roy writes that "this new brand of [post 9/11] supranational neo-fundamentalism is more a product of contemporary globalization than of the Islamic past" in terms of the "modern" global practices of the Islamic militants and even in terms of their global cultural conceptions of Islam (Roy 2002, 4). Furthermore, if we examine the position of Western Europe's approximately thirteen million Muslims we see their emergence as a strong political force based on the development of a common immigrant political identity in the face of national and/or ethnic hostility. Riva Kastoryano of the Center for International Studies and Research in Paris notes that most of these European Muslim residents have a secular background, yet "public opinion projects the difficult process of assimilating into a religion, Islam, by questioning its compatibility within the West and its ability to adopt Western 'universal' values" (Kastoryano 2002, 3). Racism takes many forms, and the Eurocentric assumption of Western universality is such a form, even though its consequences in terms of the developing international situation goes practically unrecognized.

To conceptualize the post-9/11 world, John Urry speaks of "wild zones" in the era of globalization: "Such zones possess weak states with very limited infrastructures, no monopoly of the means of coercion, barely functioning economies often dependent upon commodifying illegal materials, an imploded social structure and a relatively limited set of connections to the global order" (Urry 2003, 130). Globalization has generated such areas in the territories of the ex-USSR, across sub-Saharan Africa, in central Asia, and across the Balkans. Overwhelming military superiority can virtually obliterate nation-states such as Afghanistan and Iraq. The dispossessed from the wild zones or badlands are kept out of the homeland through racist border controls and threats of terrible retribution. The gated communities of the affluent areas in Northern and Southern cities are now matched by an attempt to produce a gated empire where only the righteous may live.

If global apartheid becomes consolidated, the issue of global governance will be reduced to a policy of isolation and repression. Just as in the big cities of the West the poor and dispossessed are marginalized in their ghettoes, so it will be on a much larger scale in the wild zones around the globe. However, capitalist globalization has led to some irreversible forms of global interconnectedness such as that provided by the Internet and electronic communications generally. What 9/11 demonstrated most clearly was that it is impossible for the dominant order to keep out the risks and the backlashes created by globalization. In the strategizing, organizing, and implementing of that operation in the imperialist heartlands, the badlands irrupted forcefully within the gated citadel. In South Africa's apartheid system it was clear at the end of the day that there was interdependence between the social/racial spheres that official ideology tried vainly and falsely to portray as separate but equal. They were neither separate nor equal.

In the mid-1990s an influential international think tank, The Group of Lisbon, produced a series of possible scenarios for the world economy. If a sustainable global integration scenario did not materialize, then a logic of fragmentation could set in. One possibility would be the apartheid scenario, although it was argued that "it is rather difficult to admit that a truly extended form of world apartheid will become a reality in the short period of twenty years" (The Group of Lisbon 1995, 83). Certainly, a "delinking" between North and South seemed unlikely, but almost ten years after this judgment was made we might not be quite so optimistic. The Group of Lisbon wrote that this scenario would "be based on a kind of cultural wall that will separate the world of the integrated and the world of the excluded" (ibid.). This we now see between the West and the world of Islam. The Group of Lisbon also argued that traditional forms of intergovernmental representation would have to become obsolete, with a "world directorate" making decisions. The contemptuous dismissal of the United Nations by the US administration in 2003 when it launched its war on Iraq seems to confirm this element. So global apartheid may not be a far-fetched nightmare scenario.

THE NEW CITIZENSHIP

If a new nonracial democracy could be built in South Africa following the collapse of apartheid, could global apartheid be replaced by a new form of citizenship? It is part of the contradictory nature of globalization that, as we have seen, it creates and fosters social divisions and injustices but also creates the conditions for the emergence of new forms of sociability. We thus see the concept of global civil society (Kaldor 2003) and that of cosmopolitan citizenship (Archibugi and Held 1996) seeking both to radicalize and to globalize our conceptions of democracy. We have seen the emergence and critique of the concept of multi-culturalism, which seeks to address the issue of ethnic diversity. The notion of equality and the rights agenda have been contested by a focus on difference. We have the tension between the quest for recognition by marginalized or oppressed groups in society and the traditional struggle for a better distribution of resources. All these debates have the questions of race and international migration at their core.

The notion of the indivisible and sovereign state is called into question by globalization, which shows how relative this is, but also by social divisions based on race, ethnicity, language, and religion. With the collapse of the master narrative of modernity, various groups have emerged demanding recognition and representation in society. Ethnic minorities, aboriginal or indigenous people, and the illegal immigrants have forcefully erupted on the political scene and ruptured the false unity of the nation-state. The nation-state of modernity is decentered, and a plurality of voices is now heard. The concept of a new citizenship emerged particularly forcefully in France during the mid-1990s to deal with a crisis in democracy in relation to immigrant rights. As Castles and Davidson note: "Members of the second generation [of North African immigrants] demanded a more participatory citizenship in a multicultural society, based on residence rather than nationality or descent" (Castles and Davidson 2000, 97). Full citizen rights in a multi-cultural democracy were now on the agenda.

Multi-culturalism seems, on the surface, an attractive and plausible model to accommodate ethnic differences (broadly understood) within a new conception of citizenship. This is a perspective that recognizes, indeed celebrates, difference, but in a one-sided way that rather assumes all differences are cultural and positive. Nor is it clear how multi-culturalism engages with the struggle for greater socioeconomic equality. The conception of identity politics it is based on is also problematic insofar as it assumes bounded identities and not the hybrid or mixed forms we find prevalent in a globalized and post-modern era. While withholding recognition from a social group (say immigrants) may be a form of oppression, it does not exhaust oppression, which is invariably complex and multifaceted. Furthermore, multi-culturalism can too often be a pluralist veneer whereby societies seek the cultural "accommodation" (read: incorporation) of immigrants and ethnic minorities.

In practice, ethnic minorities, racial groups, and immigrants often articulate their demands in terms of the so-called universal human rights rather than in the language of multi-culturalism. The postwar Universal Declaration of Human Rights provides the language and the legitimacy for claims made by a huge range of social and cultural groupings. The banner of universalism is conceived as trans-historical and cross-cultural. The rhetoric of rights is a highly influential one, but ultimately it is subordinated to that of power. It is a legalistic and a liberal conception of society that generally elides power structures and differentials. It is normative and sees the "different" category as usually lesser, the same way the mainstream version of social-exclusion theory elevates the properly "included" individual. Nevertheless, particularly through the flourishing of a universal human rights discourse in the 1990s, the rights agenda is a powerful presence on the international scene.

The question then arises, if we are to pursue the equality agenda, how that might be translated, as it were, onto the global terrain? The two concepts that come to mind are global civil society and cosmopolitan citizenship. The first is conceptualized as that sphere of international relations outside the remit of both the state and the market. It is the world of NGOs, the new social movements, and the parallel summits alongside UN gatherings on women, the environment, or racism. It is clearly a normative concept and writes out "uncivil" elements such as the Colombian drugs trade or the European neo-Nazi movement, which are equally beyond state and market. The "cosmopolitan citizen," as defined by David Held and co-authors, is "a person capable of mediating between national traditions, communities of fate and alternative forms of life" (Held et al. 1999, 449). For the cosmopolitan democracy project, the citizen of the future will enjoy multiple identities and play a mediating role with the cultures of others.

In a world that is, in reality and for the foreseeable future, quite "uncivil," global civil society seems a terrain to be valued. Against all forms of racism and xenophobia, cosmopolitanism seems an attractive alternative. And yet the limits of these discourses are plain to see. They are imbued with the values of Western liberalism and therefore are constrained in their ability to offer a planetary alternative. The conceptions of the citizen, politics, and democracy they rest on are all Western constructs. They are limited by their innate belief that liberal democracy is the "only game in town" and by their tendency to see it as an uncomplicated universal human good. As Neera Chandhoke asks, "Can global civil society transcend the existing tension between the Western world and the Third World that permeates the international legal, political, and economic order?" (Chandhoke 2002, 52). We can also ask whether the asylum seeker or refugee from an oppressive regime seeking to cross an inhospitable border identifies with the concept of cosmopolitanism.

The liberal political tradition has difficulty dealing with race issues, mainly because it draws a polite veil over the questions of imperialism and colonialism. Liberal conceptions of citizenship in Europe were irredeemably marked by the imperialist context in which they were born and the perceived need to distance themselves from the "primitive" colonial "other." The imperial order was based on an explicit and elaborate racial hierarchy of citizenship. Most peoples in the colonial world were excluded from citizenship, as were women in the West until historically quite recently. Asian immigrants to the United States remained ineligible for citizenship, even after African Americans gained the vote, purely by virtue of their color or race. In the United States, as in the UK, Catholics were deprived of the vote for a whole historical period, as were Jews, if more covertly. The liberal tradition is hardly an unambiguously inclusive one and is seriously tainted by historical and contemporary collusion with the imperialist tradition.

The colonial genealogy of citizenship as a concept and practice is evident across the Third World, not least in the late imperialist dismantling of Iraq as a state that had been artificially created by colonialism in the first place. The postcolonial states of Southeast Asia are strongly marked still by colonial structures and ideological forms. Lily Zubaida Rahim thus refers to Singapore, where the construction of a cohesive national identity goes hand in hand with "the systematic promotion of ethnic consciousness and maintenance of rigid ethnic boundaries" (Rahim 2001, 12). The colonial language of race leads to the absurdity of Sri Lankans and Pakistanis in Singapore being classified as Indians and being accorded Tamil as the mother tongue in which they are expected to be proficient. This reality of race and ethnic divisions is a long way from the lofty visions of cosmopolitanism and the strategic thinking of today's liberal imperialists supporting "humanitarian interventions" (read: wars) in sub-Saharan Africa, the Balkans, or Iraq.

So, how can we conceive of citizenship in a way that recognizes difference and equality for oppressed social groups in society? We might start by recognizing that there is always bound to be a tension between *universal* rights and the *particular* demands of diverse social groups. Universal human rights need to coexist (not always easily) with cultural relativism. But another way of framing this dilemma is to follow Todorov in arguing that the universal path passes through specific and particular cultural contexts (Todorov 1991). Diversity can be seen to be a constitutive part of universalism and not as its opposite. While the struggle against social exclusion by minority ethnic populations, for example, makes a claim for equality and against discrimination, it is also making a claim for the right to difference. Social justice requires recognition of equality before the law and respect for social and cultural differences.

CONCLUSION

This chapter has traced the various patterns of racial and ethnic divisions that underlie the broad waves of global economic, political, and cultural expansion. We have dealt with poverty patterns as articulated with race as well as with migration as an ethnicized process. We have shown that globalization is no more color blind that it is gender blind. Chua has articulated a deeply pessimistic view of the present prospects for global democracy in arguing that ultimately "markets and democracy were amongst the causes of both the Rwandan and Yugoslav genocides" (Chua 2003, 12). Free unregulated markets tend to promote and consolidate ethnic minorities, as we have seen. Democracy, in the sense of US-sponsored elections such as those in "post-liberation" Iraq and elsewhere across the majority world, also tend to consolidate minorities or unleash the pent-up resentment of majorities. In these difficult processes the shadow of colonial division is always present, and the current intervention by US imperialism is inescapable. It is indeed a "sobering lesson of globalization over the last twenty years" (Chua 2003, 16) that markets and democracy as they are currently being promoted by the architects of globalization will most likely lead to unrest, division, and at worst, genocide. But where this analysis is limited is in its restricted view of democracy, which cannot be restricted to narrow Western, let alone US notions.

Nancy Fraser argues clearly and persuasively that "redressing racial injustice . . . requires changing both political economy and culture" (Fraser 1995, 81). That is because race is at once a political economy concept (structuring deprivation and disadvantage) and a product/producer of culture in terms of racism and Eurocentrism. Whereas an equality agenda would tend toward the elimination of race as a structuring principle for socio-economic difference, a recognition agenda would seek to valorize a racialized social group's specificity. Fraser directs us to "transformative remedies" to overcome this tension, to deconstruct race and to destabilize the whole of society's sense of belonging and affiliation in keeping with the post-modern times in which we live. One way to understand what this transformative path might lead to is through the shift from gay-pride politics to contesting homophobia to the new "queer theory" politics that seek to destabilize gender identities as a whole.

7

Class, Inequality, and Exclusion

Having established that social class divisions are profoundly marked by gender and race, we now turn to the broad socio-economic parameters of class and inequality in the era of globalization. This chapter begins by exploring the polarizing dynamics of the new capitalism in terms of the haves and the have-nots in the advanced individual societies. Neo-liberalism at home in its Western bases is seen to have sharpened class inequalities even as it became the ideology behind globalization in the 1990s. It then turns to the dynamics of global inequalities and the social impact of economic inequalities outlined in Chapters 3 and 4 on the prospects for development in the South. I argue next that the best way of understanding social exclusion in the era of globalization is through a focus on local and global interactions, two domains that are often kept separate in research and policy debates. The politics of scale is seen as a key issue in how globalization is both constructed and contested. Finally (taking up themes from Chapter 5 and 6) I address the complex identities involved in social class construction and action today. Given the rise of identity politics, is it time to move beyond class?

Karl Polanyi confronted crude economistic views on social class. While he accepted that "the essential role played by class interests in social change is in the nature of things," he also argued that "the fate of classes is more frequently determined by the needs of society than the fate of society is determined by the needs of classes" (Polanyi 1957, 152). What he was referring to was the complex way in which social classes were restructured by free-market liberalism after the Industrial Revolution. With the neo-liberal globalization revolution we must likewise examine how social classes are constantly being restructured and are repositioned as part of the general social dynamic and changes in the socio-economic structure. That is, social classes must be seen as constantly in flux, in relation to one another (rather than self-sufficient), and only able to realize their own interests to the extent of their ability "to win support from outside their own membership, which again will depend upon their fulfilment of tasks set by interests wider than their own" (Polanyi 1957, 152). The question then is whether the elites or the subaltern classes will be better able to represent the general social interest to establish a sustainable form of global governance.

POLARIZING DYNAMICS

During the long postwar boom in the West it was easy to dismiss Marx's thesis of an "absolute immiseration" of the working class in contrast to the bourgeoisie steadily accumulating ever-greater profits. It appeared that there was, in fact, a general "bourgeoisification" of society, with the lower classes moving upward into a growing and increasingly affluent middle class. A polarization dynamic is one where the two extremes—at the bottom of the class ladder and at the top—receive decreasing and increasing shares of income and wealth in society. This dynamic leads to a shrinking middle ground; the middle layers either increase their share of the national income and rise economically, or they join those at the bottom of the social ladder. By around the 1960s it appeared, at least in the advanced industrial societies, that social classes were not becoming polarized. Indeed, in the 1970s and 1980s a new concept of class "fragmentation" came to the fore that seemed to undermine the whole classical conception of social classes as bounded entities. It was argued that lines of social division other than class—such as gender, race, age, sexual orientation, (dis)ability—now had primacy. Class identity was seen as a thing of the past, associated with modernism and the industrial era. The post-modern, post-industrial era would be characterized by fragmentation and a plurality of identities. Societies no longer worked on the organizing principle of class; rather, they were characterized by disorganization. There was a consensus in sociology that we needed to abandon the centrality class as an explanatory mechanism in contemporary capitalism. The emphasis was now on how a multiplicity of social cleavages interacted, producing complex and sometimes cumulative forms of exploitation and oppression.

However, by the 1990s it was evident that powerful polarizing dynamics were coming into play in most Western societies. Polarization, in relation to class analysis, is defined by Bradley as "a concentration of individuals at both ends (poles) of the class spectrum, accompanied by the widening differences in the fate of those at the top and bottom" (Bradley 1996, 208). This process of polarization was not necessarily incompatible with the ongoing dynamics of dispersion and fragmentation. Social and economic differences were, for example, always overlaid by divisions based on gender and race. The point was that capitalism was not becoming more democratic, and income differentials were not diminishing. Life chances under contemporary capitalism were still very uneven. Whereas once the ever increasing and prospering middle class was taken as a given, even by the critics of capitalism, there was now a debate on the "disappearing middle." Some from this sector became wealthy, but many, if not most, began to suffer from insecurity in employment as "downsizing" hit the corporate economy and the "flexibility" that was once seen as a problem only for blue-collar workers now began to affect white-collar employees as well.

The leading capitalist economy, the United States, is probably the exemplar of the new tendency toward polarization in class structures under globalization. For a long time it was believed that the US system, whatever its inequities, at least displayed a greater degree of class mobility than the "ossified" European nation-states. However, we must recognize how remarkably unequal the United States is today. According to Will Hutton's devastating critique of the US system, "America is the most unequal society in the industrialized West. The richest 20 percent of Americans earn nine times more than the poorest 20 percent, a scale of inequality half as great again as in Japan, Germany and France" (Hutton 2002, 187). While fully one-fifth of the US population lives in poverty, the country has some three million millionaires and the richest 1 percent of the population holds 39 percent of the total wealth. This is a polarizing dynamic at its most extreme manifestation.

It is the broader comparative picture that shows how extreme the US levels of inequality are. While the United States ranks near the top internationally in terms of per capita income, it only ranks twentieth when the income of its poorest 10 percent is compared across all advanced industrial societies. This is not a source of strength in terms of international competitiveness. Rather, as Hutton notes, "it reduces social mobility, ossifying the US into a class society as the rich gain a strangle hold on the elite educational qualifications that pave the way to the top while those at the bottom are trapped in low skills and low incomes" (Hutton 2002, 32). While the language of class divisions in the United States long has been rejected in favor of the myth of mobility in a land of opportunity, the bleak reality is more similar to that portrayed by Wolfe in *Bonfire of the Vanities,* with its polarized society consisting of two different worlds at the top and the bottom, one inside the system and the other outside of it.

The UK too has displayed strong tendencies toward polarization since the 1990s. Settlements for top executives have rocketed, and successive governments, including Labour ones, have advocated labor "flexibility" (good for capital but not usually good for workers, for whom it means poor and unstable conditions at work), supposedly to gain competitive advantage over the more socially integrationist European norm. One small illustration is the fact that in London during the 1980s (under the Thatcher government) the ratio between the income of the top decile of all households and of the bottom decile almost doubled (Castells 1996, 276). There is an argument that neo-liberal economics produces inequality but also generates possibilities for mobility. However, a broad retrospective survey of class mobility in Britain produced data and analysis that "confirm that inequalities of opportunity—at least insofar as these are measured by relative mobility chances—have not diminished to any appreciable extent throughout the largest part of the twentieth century" (Marshall, Swift, and Roberts 1997, 60). A long-term view of social class inequalities in the twentieth century shows little amelioration of disadvantage; in fact, it is sharpening under the conditions of unregulated free-market economics as advocated by neo-liberalism.

Taking a global, non-country-specific look at polarization, we should examine the dynamics of the "new" information economy. We may start from the assumption that "global communication is . . . a significant factor of equalization" (Therborn 2000, 45) in terms of people's life chances in the global economy. The technological revolution associated with information and communication technology has effectively created a network age based on dynamic innovations. However, as is also quite clear, there is now a "digital divide" between those who have access to the Internet (crucial to gain entry to the Network Age) and those who are excluded from it. So, for example, while the United States is in the clear lead in terms of overall access to the Internet, this total masks the differences between the 50 percent access for whites at the turn of the century compared to 29 percent access among African Americans and 23 percent among Hispanics. Indeed, in the late 1990s the racial divide in terms of Internet access actually widened.

So, even if we accept that increasing communication could alleviate inequalities in the global economy, we find that in practice the
"digital divide" is actually worsening them. An online survey in 2000
(cited in Castells 2001, 260–63) found that there were around 378
million Internet users worldwide (only 6 percent of the world's population), of which 43 percent were in North America, 24 percent in
Western Europe, 21 percent in Asia (including Japan), 4 percent in
Latin America, 5 percent in Eastern Europe, with the Middle East
barely surpassing 1 percent and Africa (including South Africa) not
even reaching 1 percent. If access to the new medium of communication within the whole "knowledge economy" and the networked
electronic financial system is so uneven, then clearly the prospects
for global convergence in this regard are scant. In fact, we can safely
refer to a polarizing dynamic also in terms of this new mode of development and socio-economic differentiation among classes, nations, and ethnic groups.

The new economy is not even particularly benign for those who
are included within its remit, never mind those who are socially and
culturally excluded. It is an economy where unpredictability and
instability are all-pervasive and permanent. The much vaunted
e-economy boom of the late 1990s proved as ephemeral as the South
Sea bubble of a previous "global" economic era. For workers in this
sector the norm is not a highly paid "flexible" Silicone Valley pro-
grammer but a poorly paid, probably female call-center operator
working in a third-world country. The e-economy has not provided
the definitive break with the overall capitalist tendency toward the
"deskilling" of labor. Rather, the application of digitized information technology has led to another round of debilitating degradation
of work every bit as negative for workers as the original Fordist assembly line. This time, though, the main source of workers are women
rather than men. A study of the gender and race breakdown of the
new economy and the making of a new "cybertariat" by Ursula Huws
concluded that "once again, we find that gender and race play a crucial role in determining class identity" in the new economy (Huws
2003, 176). So, neither class, gender, nor racial divisions are likely
to be overcome by the much-vaunted new economy.

In conclusion, then, work is becoming increasingly fragmented
under neo-liberal globalization, and this has arguably lessened the
importance of social class as an organizing principle. However, for
the advanced industrial societies the dominant trend over the last
decade has been one of polarization between those at the top and at

the bottom of the social scale. Castells goes even further and argues that "societies were/are becoming dualized, with a substantial top and a substantial bottom at both ends of the occupational structure, so shrinking the middle, at a pace and in a proportion that depend on each country's position in the international division of labour and on its political climate" (Castells 1996, 279). This polarization or "dualization" of contemporary class structure operates on preexisting race and gender divisions. Discrimination on the basis of race and ethnicity and in relation to migrants reinforces this pattern of increased social inequality. Gender discrimination, while less marked than it was twenty years ago, is still a negative factor, and we can further see the polarizing dynamic at work within female employment, with some women climbing the occupational ladder while many more are pushed toward the bottom.

GLOBAL INEQUALITIES

If a polarizing dynamic affects class inequality within the advanced industrial societies, what is its impact on the long-term differences between these as a group (the First World) and the developing countries (the Third World)? Dominant economic theories argue that the freeing of trade and capital flows will lead to a more efficient allocation of the world's resources. This, in turn, should help generate greater productivity and output, which leads to greater consumption. Even sharp critics of contemporary capitalism tend to accept, as Therborn does, that "increasing structural interdependence and a wider diffusion of knowledge should tend to decrease productivity differences and therefore promote the process of 'uplifting' equalization" (Therborn 2000, 37). This was certainly the pattern in Europe during the long postwar boom, and it has also been true in general for the dramatic process of agricultural modernization in East Asia since the 1970s. In brief, it cannot simply be assumed that the polarizing dynamic will prevail at a global level.

What *is* certainly the case is that increased economic integration at an international level has produced, to put it simply, losers as well as winners. Just like the mixed effects of the US boom of the 1990s (many millionaires and many more poor), international trade generates growth and dispossession, leading inevitably to increased inequality. The World Bank's argument is that global inequality has deepened because only a minority of people have participated in globalization. However, the Bank has faith that "this [current] third wave of globalization may mark the turning point at which partici-pation has widened sufficiently for it to reduce both poverty and inequality" (World Bank 2002, 7). This seems to be a flimsy basis on which to accept an optimistic scenario whereby global integra-tion will lead to a decrease in global inequality levels and a signifi-cant reduction in poverty worldwide, which is the stated objective of the World Bank and all the other international economic organiza-tions.

For some decades now it has become commonplace to assert that the North-South division is essentially obsolete. Widespread indus-trialization across what was once called the Third World has led to uneven development consolidated by the onset of globalization, which has effectively created one world. While not denying inequality at a global level, this revisionist view asserts that the core periphery dis-tinction is no longer a valid social or spatial concept. There is seen to be no overwhelming reason, other than an inability to play the "glo-balization game," why any group of countries would be disadvan-taged. However, this optimistic view is strongly contested by Arrighi and co-authors who find, on the basis of an extensive empirical study, that despite third-world industrialization "industrial convergence has not been accompanied by a convergence on the levels of income and wealth enjoyed on average by the residents of the former First and Third Worlds" (Arrighi, Silver, and Brewer 2003, 4). Table 7–1 indi-cates most clearly that in terms of conventional GNP (Gross Na-tional Product) per capita measures, the position of the Third World as a whole has not improved since 1960; indeed, the positions of Latin America and sub-Saharan Africa have significantly worsened. In conclusion, the division between rich and poor nations—the North-South divide, as it is called—remains a fundamental feature in the global dynamics of capitalism.

While it is true that uneven development has undermined the unity of the Third World (dubious at the best of times), that does not mean that convergence has been occuring at the global level between the poor and rich countries as broad groupings. Since the Second World War the developing world—mainly a postcolonial world—has struggled to mount a "development project." This was seen as re-quiring a narrowing of the industrialization gap, something that was achieved, overall, by the 1980s, if only due to de-industrialization in the North. Then, the rules of the game changed as the "globalization project" followed the national development model. Now finance capi-tal became dominant, and in this domain the Triad of the North (North

Table 7-1. GNP Per Capita for Region as Percent of First-World GNP Per Capita

Region	1960	1970	1980	1990	1999
Sub-Saharan Africa	5.2	4.4	3.6	2.5	2.2
Latin America	19.7	16.4	17.6	12.3	12.3
West Asia and North Africa	8.7	7.8	8.7	7.4	7.0
South Asia	1.6	1.4	1.2	1.3	1.5
East Asia (w/o China & Japan)	5.7	5.7	7.5	10.4	12.5
China	0.9	0.7	0.8	1.3	2.6
Third World*	4.5	3.9	4.3	4.0	4.6
North America	123.5	104.8	100.4	98.0	100.7
Western Europe	110.9	104.4	104.4	100.2	98.4
Southern Europe	51.9	58.2	60.0	58.7	60.1
Australia & New Zealand	94.6	83.3	74.5	66.2	73.4
Japan	78.6	126.1	134.1	149.4	144.8
First World**	100.0	100.0	100.0	100.0	100.0

*Countries included in Third World:
Sub-Saharan Africa: Benin, Botswana, Burkina Faso, Burundi, Cameroon, Central African Republic, Chad, Rep. of Congo, Congo Dem. Rep., Cote d'Ivoire, Gabon, Ghana, Kenya, Lesotho, Madagascar, Malawi, Mauritania, Mauritius, Niger, Nigeria, Rwanda, Senegal, South Africa, Tanzania, Togo, Uganda, Zambia, Zimbabwe
Latin America: Argentina, Bolivia, Brazil, Chile, Colombia, Costa Rica, Dominican Republic, Ecuador, El Salvador, Guatemala, Haiti, Honduras, Jamaica, Mexico, Nicaragua, Panama, Paraguay, Peru, Trinidad and Tobago, Uruguay, Venezuela
West Asia and North Africa: Algeria, Arab Rep. of Egypt, Morocco, Saudi Arabia, Sudan, Syrian Arab Rep., Tunisia, Turkey
South Asia: Bangladesh, India, Nepal, Pakistan, Sri Lanka
East Asia: Hong Kong, Indonesia, South Korea, Malaysia, Philippines, Singapore, Taiwan, Thailand
China
**Countries included in First World:
North America: Canada, United States
Western Europe: Austria, Belgium, Denmark, Finland, France, Germany, Luxembourg, Netherlands, Norway, Sweden, Switzerland, United Kingdom
Southern Europe: Greece, Ireland, Israel, Italy, Portugal, Spain
Australia and New Zealand
Japan

Source: Giovanni Arrighi, Beverly Silver, and Benjamin Brewer, "Industrial Convergence, Globalization, and the Persistence of the North-South Divide," *Studies in Comparative International Development* 38/1 (2003): 13.

America, Western Europe, and Japan) dominated. In the global re-structuring that followed, the global hierarchy of wealth between the North and South was in fact sharpened and consolidated. The legacy of colonialism and imperialism lives on in the era of global-ization as North-South divisions intensify and the ultra-imperialism of the United States opens a new era of global instability.

The globalizers have argued that countries can indeed break out of underdevelopment. One example cited is Ireland, once among the poorest of European countries and now lauded as the Celtic Tiger and a shining example for the economies of Eastern Europe now joining the European community. Interestingly, the 2001 Globaliza-tion Index survey carried out for the influential US journal *Foreign Policy* found that Ireland was at the top of the list (Foreign Policy 2002). The indicators used to construct the list included the diffu-sion of information technology, financial openness, trade openness, personal communications, and an ill-defined politics category, taken to be how "business friendly" the government was. For this study "Ireland's strong pro-business policies" have made the Irish economy "a hugely attractive location for foreign investors" (ibid., 4). Indeed, in 2000 portfolio investment flows to Ireland were the largest in the world and the pharmaceutical and information technology invest-ments by the United States in particular have transformed the Irish economy. The economy is a low tax one, and social investments are also low. For US investors it is indeed a good platform to access the European market with an educated, English-speaking, inexpensive labor force. For the population at large the investment boom has taken house prices out of the range of most people, social services are declining, and the levels of socio-economic inequality are rising. We note that while Ireland has one of the highest GDP levels in Europe, it also has one of the lowest GNP levels, reflecting the huge amount of profits repatriated by the US MNCs that deflated the GNP figures. It is estimated that two-thirds of Ireland's economic growth can be accounted for by the rise in MNC profits in the late 1990s (O'Hearn 2001, 176). A small example is the giant pharmaceutical company Pfizer, which produces Viagra in Ireland; this led to a greater than 100 percent increase in organic chemical exports from Ireland in the year 2000. This is clearly not balanced, organic, and sustain-able development of a national economy, however healthy the bal-ance sheets may look. On closer inspection, the Irish "miracle" is more of a mirage. Furthermore, it is in the very nature of this boom that it cannot be repeated, given that there is simply not that much more foreign investment waiting to create a Hungarian, Turkish, or Latvian "miracle."

However, could it not be that the poorest of the poor in the Third World have been helped by decades of development and intensive poverty-alleviation projects in recent years? For the World Bank, it is an axiom that integration with the global economy will generally reduce poverty. Examples from parts of China, parts of India, and even Vietnam are cited as proof. Nevertheless, the World Bank recognizes that in reality "there are both winners and losers from globalization" (World Bank 2002, x). Overall, the belief is that integrated economies grow faster, that growth is more widely diffused, and that this reduces poverty. From this belief springs the optimistic view that good progress is being made in meeting the target to reduce global poverty by half by the year 2011. Yet the harsh reality behind the fine words is that those living beneath the international poverty line only declined by 1 percent throughout the 1990s, a decrease from 1.3 billion to 1.1 billion. Nor was advance in the various social indicators—such as health and education—remarkable either.

It is now increasingly argued by the UNDP and other international bodies that in fact "global poverty estimates based on the $1–a-day norm are inaccurate and misleading. They under-estimate global poverty and over-estimate poverty reduction—giving a false sense of progress and unwarranted complacency" (Vandemoortele 2002, 17). It is only by ignoring this reality that optimistic statements about the inexorable way in which growth will reduce poverty continue to be produced. There is simply no good reason to assume that growth will lead automatically to poverty reduction. An anti-poverty strategy that does not explicitly bring to the fore a concern with equity will not deliver. On the other hand, as Vandemoortele argues, "from an operational point of view . . . an anti-poverty strategy that includes equity as an explicit objective can be translated into specific policy instruments—such as progressive taxation, income transfers, subsidies, elimination of user fees for basic social services, public work programmes and land reform" (Vandemoortele 2002, 13). But as none of these policy instruments are acceptable to the globalization consensus as articulated by the WTO, this is unlikely to happen.

We need, then, to consider what effect these tendencies toward polarization within the world economy have on global class structure. World system theory has for long posited that there is a global class structure over and above the nation-state system. The approach tended to collapse the spatial core-periphery or North-South divide into a social-class relationship. According to Christopher Chase-Dunn: "The world class structure is primarily composed of capitalists (owner and controller of means of production) and property-less workers. . . . [It] also includes small commodity producers . . . and a growing middle class of skilled workers" (Chase-Dunn 1998, 39). Thus the territorial division of labor is seen to "map onto" the social-class structure in a direct way. Not only is the world system granted a systematic ability to influence class formation, but the structure of class domination is perceived as already global, usually in a determinant mode vis-à-vis national, regional, and local class formations.

So can we now discern a global ruling class emerging as director and beneficiary of neo-liberal globalization? According to Leslie Sklair, "A transnational capitalist class based on the transnational corporations is emerging that is more or less in control of the processes of globalization" (Sklair 2001, 5). This social group is transnational in its composition, its lifestyle, and its perspectives or world view. While mindful of the current skepticism in regard to class theory, and even more its transferability to the global level, Sklair argues that this class "is beginning to act as a transnational dominant class in some spheres" (ibid.). It is, indeed, useful to draw attention to how transnational corporations transfer their profit-making objectives into the political arena and to understand globalization less as the pilotless machine it is sometimes portrayed as. However, we would have to integrate this level of analysis with that of politics at the nation-state level where many economic policy decisions are still taken and where political legitimacy is secured (or not) by the ruling elite.

At the other end of the global scale, we need to ask whether the transformation brought about by globalization has led to the creation of a global working class. In reality, given the immobility of labor as a rule (in spite of labor migration), the notion of a global labor market only applies to a very small layer of information-technology workers and managers. It is often forgotten that two-thirds of the world's workers are still engaged in agriculture, where there is very little tendency toward mobility. National divisions still play an overwhelming role in determining workers' perspectives, and we have racial and gender divisions as well, which make even a nationally unified working class difficult to achieve, let alone one that is acting in concert at a global level. None of this is meant to minimize, of course, those efforts that have been made by workers to engage in transnational solidarity actions (see Munck 2002); it is intended only to strike a cautious note against a view that globalization can be confronted only at the global level.

If we stand back to reflect on global inequalities in the current era, we can highlight a tendency toward polarization against the optimistic scenario portrayed by the globalizers. However, we must be cautious of working on the assumption that this is matched by a new global class structure. While globalization is indeed transforming the world around us, we cannot automatically define it as a simple causal entity in its own right. Following Urry, we note that "the global possesses systemic characteristics . . . that are distinct from those of other social systems. . . . Existing theories such as that of class domination will not work when converted to the global level" (Urry 2003, 96). That means we cannot simply scale up the nineteenth-century through early twentieth-century system of a bourgeoisie and a proletariat to the global level. The complexity of the social world we live in demands considerably more analysis and reflection before we can posit the emergence of a new global class structure and class conflict dictating the course of history.

THE LOCAL AND THE GLOBAL

Having examined the national and the global levels of class formation and socio-economic polarization we must now turn to the local level. Opponents of globalization often contrast the local to the global, investing it with the virtues of community and solidarity. Others contrast the dynamism and hyper-modernity of the global to the stasis and tradition-bound domain of the local. But in both cases there appears to be a binary opposition between the local and the global instead of a proper understanding of their dialectical relationship. In many texts on globalization the local, national, and regional levels are simply missing from the narrative. However, if we reflect on the actual making of globalization and its reproduction on a day-by-day basis, we see that it is at the local level that it takes place. It is only quite recently that global studies have become more conscious of the politics of place and that the "politics of scale" debate has brought to the fore the complex, interlinked relationships among the local, national, regional, and global dimensions of social life.

The local-global relationship is crucial to an understanding of the various social movements contesting globalization. There is a common tendency to portray the global as "outside" the domain of communities (the "inside') where social classes or groupings exist and mobilize. Thus, David Harvey, in discussing the condition of post-modernity, argues that while "movements of opposition to the disruption of home, community, territory, and nation by the restless flow of capital are legion . . . capital . . . continues to dominate, and it does so in part through superior command over space and time" (Harvey 1989, 238). Resistance movements, from this perspective, may emerge and flourish in particular places, but overall, capitalism's global historical march lies beyond their power to affect it, according to this perspective. As with Castells, there is even an attempt to conceive of capital (the economic) and labor (the social) as living in different historical times: one in a universal, virtual, instantaneous time; the other in the fragmented, nature-bound, boring clock time of everyday life. Yet the local and the global cannot really be conceived as separate spheres of social life.

The term *glocal* was adopted some time ago by Japanese corporations to signal the need to localize or ground global commodities in order to sell them better. Since then, social and cultural analysis has adapted the term *glocal* to signify the hybridity of local-global interactions. As Dirlik puts it, the term *glocal* signals the indistinguishability of local and global and "forces us to think about it as a double process at work in shaping the world: the localization of the global and the globalization of the local" (Dirlik 1999, 160). It is thus this dual or dialectical process that needs to be to the fore in any critical analysis of social class and social movement formation in the era of globalization. The local—including all its class, gender, and race divides—is at the heart of globalization's making. Conversely, there is no pristine local place where community survives intact and traditional; rather, all localities are penetrated and networked by the economic, political, and cultural moments of globalization.

On the terrain of the "glocal" there can no longer be a false opposition between the local and the global. There is, for example, no rationale for establishing a hierarchy of scales such that local is considered good and global is regarded as bad or vice versa, as happens in many popular accounts of globalization. Certainly in the anti-globalization movement there has been a tendency to prioritize the local as a terrain for transformation. Conversely, in the labor transnationalism debates (see Munck 2002, chap. 7) there has been the opposite tendency to portray all transnational labor activity as at a higher level than local or national action. David Harvey is thus skeptical of what he calls the "militant particularism" of local actions, which he even sees as close to, or tending toward fascism (Harvey 2000). Meanwhile, a whole political tradition has been built around the motto "Think globally, act locally." This view, to a greater or lesser degree, of course, tends to essentialize or naturalize the local as somehow outside of or beyond the reach of globalizing capital. Taking hybridity seriously—as symptom of the uneven but combined development of capitalism in the era of globalization—entails moving beyond such positions.

It is now becoming clear that locality and place are socially and politically constructed, as it were, in the same way that race and gender are. There is nothing natural, primordial, or given about place. Rather, as Michael Smith argues, "even the most material elements of any locality are subject to diverse readings and are given different symbolic significance by differently situated social groups and their corresponding discursive networks" (Smith 2001, 121). The social space and place of the city, for example, is socially and culturally constructed. The local of the city is hardly unitary; rather, it is contested in every possible way. Even tradition and the whole notion of authenticity as applied to a place or a city are not given but struggled over. Seattle, Barcelona, São Paulo, Sydney, Delhi, and Peking all "look different" from above (outside) and from below (inside). The complex politics of place-making cannot be reified into simple and virtuous traditions or communities seen to be standing in the way of the inexorable march of globalization.

Local politics in a global era are complex and dynamic, not reducible to a quiet backwater outside the dynamic flows of globalization. The contemporary city is shaped in every conceivable way by the forces of globalization, which it has interiorized in a way. Local urban-development strategies are inevitably global in orientation, whether it is an entrepreneurial-hierarchist strategy or one based on sustainable development. Likewise, the social claims posed in the city are local and transnational at the same time. Campaigns against racism may involve local immigrants groups and social movements, but international campaigns may also become involved. Struggles against closures of work places will seek to generate local community alliances and also forge links both "virtual" and embodied with labor and community organizations globally. As Ash Amin puts it, "Instead of seeing local political activity as unique, places might be seen as the sites which juxtapose the varied politics—local, national and global—that we find today" (Amin 2002, 397). From this perspective we might even conceive of reversing the 1970s slogan and start "Thinking locally, acting globally."

The labor movement has sought to "scale up" to meet the challenges posed by globalization, but it is not just a simple question of "going global" to match capital. The working class is embedded in particular societies and locations. It can never be as mobile as capital. While traditionally a focus on the nation-state was effective for labor to make social and political gains, that is no longer the case. The national scale is no longer the privileged arena of intervention, at least in part because its preeminence has been undermined by global economic transformations. So, labor movements have begun to take much more interest in their localities but also in the transnational context. This is a social movement that is acutely aware of how mobile and unstable the new mode of capitalist development has become. Increasingly, while "thinking locally" of what alliances hegemony can be challenged, labor as a social actor is increasingly driven to "acting globally."

What this might mean varies enormously. On the one hand, as Andy Herod notes in commenting on the 1998 General Motors strike in the United States, "in an increasingly interconnected planetary economy a locally focused campaign against a TNC [transnational corporation] may sometimes prove highly effective, particularly if such local disputes target crucial parts of that corporations global operation" (Herod 2001, 412). This would be a global strategy, in terms of the strategic visions, but one applied locally. In other cases, local disputes such as the Liverpool and Australian dock strikes of the late 1990s (see Kennedy and Lavalette 2003) can reach out to dockers internationally to build solidarity action. These strikes also built strong community support, but they saw the advantage to be gained from transnational action. So, simply empowering the local as a counter to globalization makes little sense in the context of these examples of the new labor internationalism. Rather, capital's "glocal" strategy calls for a "glocal" response from the subaltern social classes and the social movements they generate.

A graphic representation of this complex interaction among the levels of society can be obtained from Figure 7–1.

Figure 7–1. Socio-Spatial Matrix

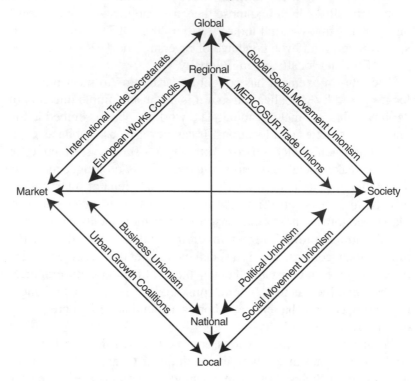

The various points of the diamond should be conceived of as poles of attraction setting up force fields affecting the activity of labor in complex and interrelated ways. Workers and labor movements operate within the parameters of the market, but they are also embedded within social relations. So we can see, for example, how a business unionism is closer to the logic of the market than, say, a social-movement unionism, which is more attuned to the needs of society, or even a political unionism that still operates within the parameters of the nation-state. Then, without posing a hierarchy, labor actions can also be seen to have a spatial dimension, ranging from the local community level to the global transnational space that has its official and unofficial sub-spaces. The International Trade Secretariats operate more in a market-dominated force field than the newer social-movement unionism oriented organizations, for example. Then, the regional scale of union activity can show a more market-oriented repertoire of action and approach (European Works Councils) or a more social orientation, as with the MERCOSUR union alliance among the Brazilian, Argentinean, Paraguayan, and Uruguayan labor movements. At the local or city level, unions may participate in the urban growth coalitions that many cities engaged in the race toward "competitiveness" have developed, or they may adopt a more social-movement orientation toward the broader community and its complex issues. I would argue, in conclusion, that neither axis of social formation and political action is self-sufficient; it is their combined and uneven effects that shape the contemporary workers' movement.

We can thus see how the parameters of social transformation in today's world are complex and not reducible to any slogans, in fact. Central to any progressive strategy is a proper understanding of the fluid and dynamic way in which a new "politics of scale" is being forged. Traditional divisions between local and global, regional and national, home and locality are all being socially reconstructed by what we call globalization, which is a complex cluster of processes, as we have seen. The start of the twentieth century was, following Sallie Marston's review of the social construction of scale, "a period of substantial economic, political and spatial transformations as new social—gender, race, class—relations were being wrought around an emergent form of mature industrial corporate capitalism" (Marston 2000, 235). A similar period of reconstruction is occurring at the start of the twenty-first century as a new globalized networked-information society is consolidated. From the household, through the locality, to regional, national, and global scales of social life, much is being renegotiated and recast, including the traditional or modern-era relations of social class, gender, and race.

Globalization has led to a restructuring of scale as a social relation. There is no fixed ontological status to what we term *local* and *global*. Social relations are stretched across time and space, while the time-space relation is compressed with the increased velocity of all flows. As Ash Amin puts it (following Jessop): "The combined outcome is a proliferation of scales and scalar complexity rather than a simple replacement of national scales by a global scale of action" (Amin 2002, 387). This is a conclusion that must inform our analysis of how social exclusion can be contested in the era of globalization. It is certainly not a case of simply switching from a national model of politics and welfare to a global one. While we must recognize the importance of the emerging global scale of social activity, we must also bear in mind all of the "new" regionalisms, the "new" localisms, and the ongoing gender contestation of the household.

COMPLEX IDENTITIES

Traditionally, social classes were viewed as broad socio-economic groupings with shared cultural and political characteristics that sought to transform society in their image. The bourgeois vision of society was opposed by the proletarian perspective that essentially looked forward to a classless future. Today, we are usually seen to live in a post-class (if not classless) society in which life chances are dictated by the intersection of a multiplicity of status and identity divisions or differences. Against the economism that lay at the heart of traditional modernist conceptions of social class, we now stress non-class differences such as age, gender, and race in shaping who we are and how we react to events around us. Our lifestyles and values are not dictated solely (or even) by our economic role in society, but rather by our identity, which we like to think we choose for ourselves. This may well be a Western conceit, but it explains, to a large extent, why the language of class, and in particular class conflict, has given way to the aspirations of individualism.

A major feature of neo-liberal economics is precisely its emphasis on the individual, but it is one shared with certain complacent versions of post-modernism that also celebrate the individual and a greater freedom of action. People can supposedly choose to belong to any given identity group. Individuals, not society, choose their correct identity and thus set down roots and build a vision of where they want to go in life. Identity politics have flourished since the 1980s (at least in the West) as social class (where it had prevailed) broke down as a significant or meaningful category. However, we must consider carefully historian Eric Hobsbawn's view that identity politics are more a symptom of social breakdown than a solution: "Identity politics and fin-de-siécle nationalism were . . . not so much programmes, still less effective programmes for dealing with the problems of the late twentieth century, but rather emotional reactions to these problems" (Hobsbawn 1994, 43). From this perspective an identity politics is inimical to social transformations insofar as it is based on exclusion (to be included requires saying who is excluded), and alliances are inevitably fickle if not based on an overall vision of societal change.

When identity politics first emerged, it was largely under the sign of a critique of class "essentialism" and a recognition that classes were "gendered" and "racialized." In complex societies it was pointless to seek to reduce social divisions to an overarching class paradigm based mainly on economic function. Post-modernism, in a loose sense of the term, spelled fluidity, and it tended to stress the "unfixity" of social identity. Deconstruction of stable identities would lead to a flourishing of diversity. However, what Hobsbawn points to is a confluence toward the end of century between this perspective and many "fundamentalisms" seeking new "essences" to use as anchor in the rapid flows of post-modern globalism. Ethnic identity politics can, for example, be seen precisely as a way of responding to the deconstruction of fixed identity. The language of authenticity and a certain cultural absolutism began to take over from earlier stress on diversity and pluralist democracy.

If we refuse to choose between class politics and identity politics, then we are driven to explore the complexity of social life and identity under contemporary capitalism. Perhaps the greatest problem to be overcome in developing an adequate class analysis is the tendency in quantitative sociology toward nominalism, that is, social class as simply a property of individual cases. From a complexity viewpoint, as Byrne concludes, we would rather see class "as an emergent phenomenon which is the product of the interactions of its component parts. It has a reality over and beyond any individual component and has causal powers which do not derive from the properties of the components taken separately" (Byrne 1999, 76). All of an individual's identities come into the equation, but the individual is also part of a complex whole. Societies are complex, and social classes take diverse forms not reducible to income alone. Above all, against the nominalist tradition, social classes should not be conceived of as entities (with names attached) but rather as the result of processes such as informalization, globalization, informationism, feminization, racialization, flexibilization, and so on, as we have seen.

Class, then, clearly affects gender and race processes as well as being shaped by them. As Bradley notes: "Classes are not only divided by gender: they are 'gendered' in the sense that gender is integral to processes of class formation, action, and identification" (Bradley 1996, 74). The sexual division of labor lies at the heart of capitalist development and class formation. Gender differences—portrayed as natural by patriarchal science and law—often serve to underpin and legitimize class divisions. Gendered ideologies are also used to justify the predominant role of white men in global power structures. On the other hand, class differences do divide women, maybe increasingly so as polarizing dynamics lead to some women benefiting from globalization while many more suffer the increasing feminization of poverty. The divisions between first-world and third-world women are also crucial, as are those between white women and women of color. Gender is central to the making of social class and vice versa.

Racial and ethnic divisions also cut across the class structures and help shape them. As with gender, supposedly natural ethnic differences (in fact, socially constructed, of course) are used to legitimize class inequalities as in the United States and elsewhere. Conversely, following Anthias and Yuval-Davis, "at the same time, class processes are involved in the racialization of particular social/ethnic categories" (Anthias and Yuval-Davis 1993, 18), most notably with the racialization of third-world migrant workers. Social-class divisions are shaped by and in turn affect ethnic differences. Racism is used as a means to divide the subaltern classes and to provide cohesion for ruling groups against the "other" or outsiders. From the open exploitation of slavery and colonialism to the more coded yet insidious ethnic and racial divisions in today's advanced capitalist countries, white men have exploited people of color. Globalization, increased economic integration, and a degree of cultural hybridity have all influenced the race/class interactions, and not always positively.

The dynamics of inequality in contemporary capitalism are both generated and perpetuated by the class structure. Social identities may be multiple and certainly not reducible to economic position in society, but social class is still a key determinant of life chances. We also need to introduce consumption into the equation, along with production, to understand how social groupings are formed in society. Some social groups—such as the underclass—appear to be outside the class structure, but this may be questionable. The centrality of the labor/capital relation may not be obvious in the era of finance capital, but we still have to produce the food and the goods we need to survive. So, in conclusion, we can question the widespread assumption that class divisions or even class awareness is declining. Following Jonathan Rutherford, "Class is still a conceptual necessity for understanding the dynamics of society . . . [even if] the restructuring of its processes and the decline of old class identities and cultures has coincided with a proliferation and dispersal of other political and social antagonisms" (Rutherford 1990, 12). To put it bluntly: class matters.

When we turn from the West to the rest of the world, we find that identities are equally complex but that other overarching divides and identities come to the fore. Neither gender nor community, the state, or democracy mean or signify the same thing under Islam as they do in the West. While Islam is fragmented both spatially and culturally, it does offer a perspective on globalization radically at odds with Western (including critical) perspectives. While the understanding of *umma* (togetherness) varies among the world's billion Muslims, it does provide a shared identity and a common bond against the fragmentation and relationization of Western cultural globalization. While during the period of colonialism many Islamic countries, or at least leaderships, adopted the Western development model, there is now, at least since the 1978 overthrow of the Shah in Iran, a decisive move against Western development and political models. Since the Gulf Wars of 1991 and 2003 the project of creating Islamic solidarity against all things Western appears to be an attractive and rational project. From a Western perspective the only "modern" Islam is one that takes on Western values, but that is not how the world is viewed from a traditional, never mind fundamentalist, Muslim perspective.

Certainly we cannot reduce the "meaning" of Islam to opposition to globalization as though Islam were just another, anti-globalization movement. Rather as Mustapha Kamal Pasha argues, we might better "attempt to see globalization and Islamism as mutually constitutive" and thus avoid "the perils of binary constructions of contradictory phenomena" (Pasha 2002, 130). From this perspective it becomes clear how fundamentalism feeds on globalization in so many ways. Following the dictates of neo-liberal global economic order reduces the capabilities of any secular or nationalist state to deliver basic necessities to its population. Integration into the unfolding narrative of globalization spells cultural homogenization and acceptance of the "one best way" (a Western way). The emerging alternative of an Islamic democracy is thus increasingly attractive. Yet this alternative, as Pasha writes, "assumes a more rejectionist, and often illiberal, profile given its marginalization within a globalizing context— spurned, mocked, and attacked as an symbol of barbarity or social pathology" (Pasha 2002, 131). Whatever the outcome of this ongoing conflict, it will not be one where Western globalization will have carried out its self-proclaimed mission of taking democracy to less fortunate peoples and nations.

What the example of Islam brings into the debate is, inevitably, the question of imperialism in the age of globalization. There can be no greater form of social exclusion than that which excludes whole regions of the world because they fail to "integrate" with the world economy. As with the racialized language of much immigration discourse, the onus is now placed on the "other" to assimilate. Whole histories of development in the non-West are obliterated as though these are simply empty spaces waiting to be integrated into the onward march of history. This march is being conducted to the hymns of innate Western superiority in every domain of human life and endeavor from the economic to the political, from the cultural to the moral and religious. With the effective recolonization of much of the non-Western world—most clearly in Afghanistan and Iraq, of course, but also in Latin America—a new overarching social division is being constructed. Whether we call it globalization, imperialism, or Americanization is less important than considering and acting upon its overwhelming impact on life chances in the non-West.

CONCLUSION

This chapter has examined various facets of socio-economic class divisions in the era of globalization. The first two sections argued that the dominant dynamic is not one in which class divisions become more diffuse but rather a process of class polarization occurring both between nations (the North/South axis) and within nations. We also explored the complex dynamic of local/global relations in terms of class formation and mobilization. This politics of scale needs to be added to our Polanyi-inspired theme of market/society relations as the overarching divide in contemporary politics. Finally, the complex nature of class and non-class identities was explored. Class still matters, indeed, but always taken in conjunction with a gendered/racialized/culturalist dynamic. Class may constitute gender relations, but the reverse is also true.

Class is better conceived as a social process rather than as a bounded social grouping. Most sociological and Marxist conceptions of class tend to view capitalism as a social totality. As Gibson-Graham explains, this has the unfortunate effect of allowing capitalism "to take up all the available social space, incorporating the noneconomic dimensions of social life such as culture and politics as well as noncapitalist economic realms such as household production" (Gibson-Graham 1996, 57). It is actually impossible to conceive of a process of global social transformation today from a purely economic viewpoint. Culture, religion, ethnicity, and gender are always present in the making of this globalized world and in the various projects to make a more participative future possible. In households, communities, and even at the nation-state level the "commodification" of social life under neo-liberalism is being contested on a daily basis. That, I believe, is the message of Polanyi when he argues that "mere class interest cannot offer, therefore, a satisfactory explanation for any long-run social process" (Polanyi 1957, 152–53).

8

Beyond Social Exclusion

Ultimately, as Karl Polanyi wrote in the middle of the twentieth century, "the control of the economic system by the market is of overwhelming consequence to the whole organization of society: it means no less than the running of society as an adjunct to the market" (Polanyi 1957, 57). The crucial question today is whether society can regulate the free market in the interests of humanity or not. This leads us to the emerging problematic of "global governance," whereby multilateral economic institutions seek some political legitimacy for the globalization project and set up social safety nets to deal with the social exclusionary effects of globalization. But is this simply a form of social control? The meaning of all these terms is hotly contested in this regard, most obviously with the term *globalization* itself, for example, not to mention *democracy*. Social movements also emerge, contesting globalization in practice and seeking to "re-embed" the market in society, as Polanyi had originally advocated. And, finally, we need to explore social inclusion as the opposite of social exclusion, but also ask whether this is enough. A transformative approach to globalization and its discontents would arguably be better served through the empowerment of all socially excluded peoples, social groups, and nations. But what would that mean in practice, and how might it be achieved? These are the political issues that we turn to in this final chapter that acts as a conclusion but also opens up a whole new agenda "beyond" social exclusion. As Craig Murphy puts it, "The best arguments for paying attention to the world polity are ethical and moral" (Murphy 2000, 789).

MARKETS AND SOCIETY

"The global sweep of economic liberalism can now be taken in at a glance. Nothing less than a self-regulating market on a world-scale could ensure the functioning of this stupendous mechanism" (Polanyi 1957, 138). Thus Karl Polanyi in 1944 described the rise of economic liberalism, but it is only now that this project is beginning to be fully materialized. Globalism, as a capitalist project, seeks nothing other than a self-regulating market on a global scale. As in Polanyi's day, this cannot be achieved by simply allowing things to take their course. In that sense the economic doctrine of laissez faire was not in practice a question of "let it be" but, rather, of state *imposed* "free markets." As Polanyi put it: " There was nothing natural about laissez faire; free markets could never have come into being merely by allowing things to take their course. . . . The road to the free market was opened up and kept open by an enormous increase in continuous, centrally organized and controlled interventionism" (Polanyi 1957, 139–40). Today the IMF, the WTO, and national governments seek to impose laissez faire though strong-arm tactics against developing countries' trading prospects and to keep all legal and social impediments to capital's free rule firmly under control. But, can this capitalist utopia (or to be precise, distopia) actually be achieved?

For Polanyi, while the market expanded continuously, this tendency was checked by a countermovement of society: "This was more than the usual defensive behaviour of a society faced with change; it was a reaction against a dislocation which attacked the fabric of society, and which would have destroyed the very organization of production that the market had called into being" (Polanyi 1957, 130). Thus, in practice, during the postwar period the free market and the laissez faire state were replaced, across the West, by regulated markets (the "mixed economy') and interventionist states. This set of processes represented, in an admittedly abstract way, society regulating the market. Markets, following Polanyi, could not be totally "disembedded" from society and politics. The welfare state—albeit unevenly implemented across the West—meant that labor was not just a simple commodity (as Polanyi from a Christian-socialist perspective had stressed) and that welfare measures would seek to create nationally embedded markets in a compromise between capital and labor.

Two key watchwords of contemporary capitalism—*competition* and *flexibility*—conspire against such a stable socially embedded market system today. As the Group of Lisbon notes: "Competitiveness has become the primary goal of industrialists, bankers, and governmental trade and industry departments. Industrialists, politicians,

economists, financial leaders, technologists, and trade unionists have
adopted the competitiveness metaphor as their credo" (The Group
of Lisbon 1995, 91). Competition today is seen as the driving force
for democracy (elections are about competition, after all) and competitiveness has become the altar on which all ethical and moral values are sacrificed. Competitiveness at a national level can operate as
a spurious excuse to ignore human needs and human rights. Competition can be healthy, certainly, but it can also lead to economic wars,
not to mention the loss of jobs and the reduction of living standards
that it invariably creates. What competition cannot deliver, however,
is long-term sustainable growth or stable governance, both of which
demand a level of balanced growth and long-term vision that the
ideology of competitiveness is plainly at odds with.

The other major principle of neo-liberal globalization is that of
flexibility, so important that we can now be said to live in the era of
"global labour flexibility" (Standing 1999). As with competition,
flexibility can indeed be seen as a virtue. Companies need to be flexible and so also must governments and even national societies. Work
could be more enjoyable and rewarding if it were more flexible.
However, what flexibility in practice means for the world's workers
is insecurity and precarious working environments. For companies,
flexibility means the freedom to hire and fire at will, or to lower
wages in pursuit of competitiveness. Flexibility is advocated as a
counter to bureaucracy, but what it actually operates against is social
cohesion and inclusion. In this vein it is clear that flexibility operates in tandem with competitiveness, with its short-term consider-
ations of private profit operating to the detriment of social inclusion
and sustainable democracy.

It is important to note at this stage that capitalism is not moving
inexorably toward some predefined end state in which markets rule
supreme. Notions such as the end of history have been shown to be
hopelessly utopian. Fukuyama's bold thesis on the end of history
(Fukuyama 1993) struck a certain chord in the early 1990s following the collapse of the Berlin Wall and the communist regimes shortly
thereafter. Borrowing from Marx's intellectual mentor Hegel for his
philosophical underpinnings, Fukuyama argued confidently and categorically that our social and political horizons were set by the definitive and final end of the liberal capitalist order. No other alternative was possible, and resistance was futile. All projects for
comprehensive social and political transformation should simply accept the end of history as an open-ended or non-teleological process.

Within a few years this dream/nightmare was disproved categorically by the Islamic challenge to Western hegemony, wars of conquest and wars over scarce resources, and the somewhat unexpected rise of a counter-globalization (or capitalism) movement. In terms of social and political theory we have also moved beyond such crass denials of social conflict, history, and the ever-present options of alternative scenarios for human progress.

If we take a Polanyian view of a long-term history, we see that there have been cycles in the market's relationship with society and vice versa. It was only toward the end of the eighteenth century that there was a decisive move by the state to disembed capitalist development and economic behavior from society and politics. The British New Poor Law of 1834 marked symbolically the triumph of the market as labor became effectively a commodity and disembedding prevailed. Then, toward the end of the nineteenth century, the self-regulating market entered a crisis culminating in the Wall Street collapse of 1929, the Great Depression, and the rise of fascism in the 1930s. From this crisis sprang the compromise welfare state and social re-embedding of the market in the postwar period. Recently, we find disembedding prevailing since the 1980s, challenged more recently from within by the more lucid supporters of globalization, and from without by a range of social and political forces.

Many issues today are leading to a renegotiation of market-society relations, and there are indications that many have heeded Polanyi's warning that "a market economy can function only in a market society" (Polanyi 1957, 57). First of all, there is a growing recognition in the corridors of global power that the inequalities generated by the prevailing market system matter, over and beyond moral or political concerns. For the UNDP, inequality has many negative effects. It can

- exacerbate the effect of market and policy failure on growth;
- erode social capital, including the sense of citizen responsibilities needed to build public institutions;
- increase a society's tolerance for inequality (UNDP 2002, 17).

In these different but interrelated ways we see how inequality actually matters in terms of sustainable capitalist development. The first element is crucial in economic terms because it acts as an obstacle to growth in developing (usually more unequal) economies and limits the opportunities for more and wider layers of society to be absorbed

into capitalist relations. Even the policies of neo-liberal globalization require some social regulation over the market's inherent tendency to create inequality.

In the second place, we are seeing a growing recognition that capitalism itself loses something essential to its well-being when it em-
braces the free-market credo uncritically. Francis Fukuyama, who
saw the end of history coming after the collapse of the Soviet Union
(Fukuyama 1992), was by the mid-1990s writing another mood-
catching text on the social virtues of trust (Fukuyama 1996) and the
need to recapture them. Indeed, it is ironic that at the very moment
of capitalism's triumph, it began to lose the virtues that had allowed
it to prosper. Trust, but also honor and respect, was not something
confined to the pre-capitalist part but an integral part of how capitalism operated. Inter-capitalist relations on a daily business basis require a degree of trust, but the free market, unregulated by social (let
alone moral) values, cannot generate this. The US-UK model of rampant neo-liberalism—as exemplified by the Enron scandal, among
others—has been particularly prone to this weakness compared to
the European and Japanese models, which tend to retain some of
these "old" values.

Finally, we are seeing, at least since the East Asian financial crises of 1987–88 a recognition that markets cannot manage capitalism
on their own. Markets are imperfect, and they fail, even in terms of
their own logic. Markets produce pollution, and they do not create
sustainable growth. Markets are susceptible to ups and downs (contrary to the belief that the Wall Street boom of the 1990s would go
on forever), and this leads to slumps and depressions. Joseph Stiglitz,
from within the managing circles of global capitalism but a critic of
free-market fundamentalism, argues that "government can, and has,
played an essential role not only in mitigating these market failures
but also in ensuring *social justice*. Market processes may, by themselves, leave many people with too few resources to survive" (Stiglitz
2002, 218). In the nineteenth and most of the twentieth centuries the
main danger to people from the market was famine, which devastated Ireland, India, China, and Africa. Now, the main danger of the
market lies in the financial sector of "casino capitalism" that, unregulated, can generate a crisis of devastating effect that can spread
rapidly across continents.

Polanyi's perspective allows us to bring society back into the debate on how globalization may be built and prosper on a stable basis.
The market economy must be socially embedded to be stable, and it

must be socially regulated to be sustainable. Polanyi saw the fundamentalist liberal ideologies of the 1920s as at least partly responsible for the rise of fascism in the 1930s. Polanyi would not be sur-
prised by the tremendous drive of free-market fundamentalists today
and the dangers they pose for world peace and prosperity. What is
interesting, politically, is how Polanyi offers a way out from the
cul de sac of socialist politics as we have known them, namely the
Soviet-statist model. For Polanyi, "Socialism is, essentially, the
tendency inherent in an industrial civilization to transcend the self-
regulating market by consciously subordinating it to a democratic
society" (Polanyi 1957, 234). While a radical departure from current
institutional debates on governance, on the one hand, and the anti-
capitalist movement, on the other hand, this is also a simple and
sensible strategy to counter the ill effects of globalization.

While Polanyi's framework of analysis offers inspiration for a
strategy of transformation—or radical reform—it does suffer from
two problems. The first is Polanyi's under-specified and somewhat
voluntaristic notion of societal reaction to the free market. It is never
entirely clear how or even why this might occur. It can hardly be
spontaneous or a natural reaction to free-market excesses. Nor is
there an automatic tendency for democracy to expand universally
without political struggle. These weaknesses are understandable,
given Polanyi's lack of direct political involvement, unlike his contemporary Antonio Gramsci, who engaged with similar issues. The
other limitation is historical, namely, the assumption that "society"
would react only at the national or local level. While Polanyi could
see the global making of free-market liberalism through the *haute
finance* sector, he thought the social countermovement would be based
on national societies, which would also set the parameters of their
programs and political ambitions. We cannot start from this assumption in today's global age. Clearly, global social exclusion can only
be tackled by global social regulation. If the Polanyi perspective is
globalized and "operationalized" by specifying the social and political forces that will tackle free-market fundamentalism, then it can
serve to set the broad parameters of the task ahead.

GOVERNANCE AND CONTROL

The logic of the above discussion is that capitalist markets require
a system of global governance to regulate them and secure the interests of society. As the World Commission on the Social Dimension

of Globalization notes: "Up till now the increasing international attention to issues of governance has been almost exclusively focused on the national level. The issue of global governance now warrants serious attention. Global governance is the system of rules and institutions established by the international community and private actors to manage political, economic and social affairs" (World Commission on the Social Dimension of Globalization 2003, no. 335, 97). It seems almost as if it is becoming necessary to save globalization from itself as much as from its enemies. With the global system far more complex and interdependent than it was, say in the 1980s, a degree of governance is deemed necessary by all but the most fundamentalist of free marketers. Given that the global system is more complex now than it ever was, that governance needs to influence all levels of human activity, from the local to the global, and cannot rely simply on national economic and social policies. With power now more diffuse than in the heyday of the nation-state, Hollingsworth suggests that "there is slowly evolving a set of institutions for the governance of societies at multiple levels, but this process is poorly understood and its long-term consequences are rarely discussed" (Hollingsworth 2004, 56). The main issue to be discussed here is whether global governance is a force for democratization or an agent of social control.

Globalization and governance came to the fore around the same time in the mid-1990s, and that is hardly surprising. Traditional forms of governance focused on the nation-state were no longer adequate in a world where many issues were now transnational, from the environment to financial regulation, from labor standards to property rights. The globalization and governance debate thus began, focused on the need to reform international institutions and, if necessary, to create new ones. While economic regulation of the new transnational order fell squarely into the hands of the WTO, global social regulation was a more contested terrain. On the one hand, there was the neo-liberal so-called iron triangle of the WTO, World Bank, and IMF; on the other hand, there were the more "social" organizations of the United Nations, from the UN's own Department of Economic and Social Affairs, to the UNDP, the ILO, and the World Health Organization. While the neo-liberal mainstream saw no need for social regulation of the new economic order, the "UN family" organizations pointed to a range of new transnational policy issues.

Among these pressing demands, Bob Deacon focuses on the need

- to preserve and improve labour standards
- to establish a global set of social policy principles
- to regulate the emerging international markets in private health, education and social protection
- and to establish guidelines for corporate social responsibility (Deacon 2003, 2–3).

Each of these issues is contested vigorously between the reformers (radical or otherwise) and those who simply seek to apply a cosmetic social facade to cover the underlying neo-liberal deregulating agenda. Thus the transnational corporations would contest any attempt to regulate medical products and health needs, as seen in the dispute over the production of generic HIV/AIDS medications. Likewise, various attempts to establish corporate social responsibility, such as the UN's Global Compact, have been criticized for merely burnishing business images. There is also a tension with third-world governments that, often rightly, see social regulation (for example, of labor standards) as a covert way of promoting Northern competitiveness in the global economy.

There is, however, a wide range of organizations that are now supportive of the notion of global governance. Most influential has been the Commission on Global Governance, whose influential report *Our Global Neighborhood* was published in 1995. It acknowledged that the needs of effective governance were now beyond the capabilities of national governments. It called for a multifaceted strategy for global governance and highlighted the need to set up a complex process of interactive decision-making at all levels of globalization. There was much talk at this time of global citizenship and the need to include the poor and the marginalized sectors of society in the governance process. But, ultimately, the report argued quite uncritically that most often "governance will rely primarily on markets and market instruments, perhaps with some institutional oversight" (The Commission on Global Governance 1995, 5). This apparent retreat from the lofty ideals of global citizenship to embrace market fundamentalism explains why many observers are skeptical of the whole notion of global governance.

More recently, in 2003, the World Commission on the Social Dimensions of Globalization carried out an intensive investigation across the world sounding out opinions of the "social partners" employers, trade unions, and community groupings, as well as a number of governments. Its report is both comprehensive and a lucid statement of the reformist argument. Its conclusions are illuminating in regard to the contradictory aims and methods of the global governance approach. On the one hand it argues that "Good governance . . . should further values such as freedom, security, diversity, fairness and solidarity. It should also ensure respect for human rights, international rule of law, democracy and participation . . . (World Commission on the Social Dimensions of Globalization 2003, no. 335, 97). Certainly some of these terms, such as "freedom," can be interpreted in different ways, but overall this is an unambiguously democratic global agenda. But then the sentence is completed with the other values that need to be respected: " . . . promote entrepreneurship and adhere to the principles of accountability, efficacy and subsidiarity" (ibid.). Here in a nutshell is the neo-liberal economic efficiency model enshrined as a basic human good. At least there must be some tension between promoting the "entrepreneurship" of the MNCs and financial speculators and maintaining respect for basic human rights.

One could develop an analogy between this ambiguous impact of governance with the process of "decarceration" and current moves to deal with crime in a more "social" manner. In *Visions of Social Control* Stanley Cohen argued that exclusion and social control are no longer the only ways to deal with deviance. The deviant can, rather, be reintegrated into society through much more insidious forms of inclusionary control. For Cohen: "In order to include rather than exclude, a set of judgments has to be made which 'normalizes' intervention in a greater range of human life" (Cohen 1985, 115). This is precisely what is occurring with global governance that entails a much greater state involvement with all spheres of social life. Social control can take much more diffuse and subtle forms than the prison, and in the same way the poor and marginalized may be controlled in more effective ways than brutal social and political exclusion. In a similar way work places are now dominated by rigid work practices but allied with a "softer" more subtly implemented "human relations" approach.

The theme of governance as a new form of social control can also be pursued in relation to Antonio Gramsci's concept of "transformism." For Gramsci, writing about Italy in the period of modernization, transformism is a way of exercising hegemony in the dominant socio-economic groups deal with a crisis in a defensive way. This mode of domination involves a gradual absorption and cooptation of antagonistic groups in society (Gramsci 1971, 59). While, for example, a dominant or hegemonic class may be transforming society, it is simultaneously engaging in restoration of the old order. Thus, global governance can be seen as a means to coopt groups antagonistic to the new global order. Transformism, following Gramsci, is a type of passive revolution in which a bland consensus is formed (for example, the desirability of a global neighborhood) that effectively neutralizes active opposition and divides it.

As a contemporary paradigm we have Foucault's emphasis on "governmentality" to describe the process of self-reliant networks of governance we now see emerging and consolidating (Foucault 1977). Contemporary socio-political transformations under the aegis of governance are supposed to signal the triumph of the people over the state. The state is being "hollowed out," and people are becoming active in networks of government through which they become empowered. Where once there was an emphasis on centralization, we now see a stress of decentralization. Power now seems much more diffuse than in the heyday of bureaucratic industrial capitalism. However, it is probably more accurate to see global governance not as the disappearance of social power but rather its extension to new domains (see Douglas 1999). Global governance can be seen as the most modern practice of social power, another Western vision for the world, every bit as domineering as colonialism or imperialism.

While I think we need to accept the possible underlying suspicions of the negative or skeptical view of global governance, I would like to explore, here, a rather more nuanced and optimistic approach. First of all, we could argue that the main problem with the global-governance debate is that it focuses on policies and not politics. It is the narrowness of the options and the attempt to restrict these to technical choices not political ones that are the main problems. Thus bringing politics back into the governance debates could make it a fruitful terrain of struggle. In the second place, against all conspiratorial views—for example, "the iron fist in the velvet glove" thesis—which grant a seamless unity to power politics, we should be more tuned in to differences and, arguably, the more porous nature of governance compared to traditional governmental forms of rule. Finally, we should be quite conscious that the realistic option to the current terrain of global governance is not a global uprising of the oppressed but, rather, the empowerment of the imperial US rogue state that would prefer to dispense with all UN niceties of governance.

Pursuing this more policy-oriented rather than critique-focused interpretation we can see to what extent global governance is actually being contested today. Since the mid-1990s a whole range of NGOs and global social movements have engaged with the various global-governance organs. They have long had influence in the UN "family," but more recently the women's movement has had a significant impact on the World Bank's gender policies as well, for example. The environmental movement has also made significant inroads with the WTO, and even the IMF has seen fit to engage in dialogue with the international labor movement. This social engagement with the bodies in charge of global economic management has certainly been uneven. It also has its limit insofar as third-world organizations committed to alternative development models will simply not be "heard" compared to an organization such as Oxfam, for example, which basically accepts the optimistic vision of neoliberal globalization and engages in a "professional" dialogue. Nevertheless, governance is not simply about cooption.

We could go further and note that global governance is not only continuously contested but actually leads to a globalization of social conflict. As Nicola Yeates argues: "Globalization has thrown up structures for contestation, resistance and opposition which mediate the process and effects of globalization and create space for an alternative politics of globalization" (Yeates 2001, 28). The parameters of global governance could be expanded following this approach to go beyond the narrow institutional definition that prevails. Global governance is about much more than simply scaling up the welfare state to the global level to deal with the social exclusion generated by globalization. It is about global politics and what type of world we want to live in. It is about the nature of the economic system that is now developing, its emphasis on competitiveness over human welfare, and its supreme indifference to cultural diversity and different conceptions of human development.

DISCOURSE AND CONTESTATION

What should be clear by now is that all the terms in the debates we have entered are contested, both discursively and in practice (although these two cannot really be separated, as we shall see). When the World Bank refers to *globalization* or *empowerment* these terms do not mean the same as they do to a grass-roots organization, say, in India. When the counter-globalization or an opposition group under a repressive regime calls for democracy, it does not mean the same as when the US government calls for democratization. Amy Chua, who writes on the rise of ethnic conflicts worldwide and the failure of Western democracy to deal with the issues, writes scathingly that "when Americans call for world democratization, we don't mean world democracy. For Americans, global democratization means democracy for and within individual countries. . . . The last thing most Americans want is a true world democracy, in which our economic and political fate is determined by a majority of the world's countries or citizens" (Chua 2003, 260). Even that particular democracy-for-each-country model is based on a firmly "made in (and friendly to) the USA" conception of what democracy means. What is also clear now is why the global-governance agenda appears progressive with such ethno-centric and self-centered notions being promoted. But the main point to make is that an assumed human good such as global democracy is far from agreed upon across that globe of supposedly democratic nations and peoples.

To clarify the implications of this disjuncture we can start with Michel Foucault, who dealt most effectively with the power-knowledge relationship from a transformationalist perspective. For Foucault, "Power and knowledge directly imply one another . . . [and] . . . there is no power relation without the correlative constitution of a field of knowledge, nor any knowledge that does not presuppose and constitute at the same time power relations" (Foucault 1977, 27). The discourses of development, globalization, social exclusion, social capital, and others we have dealt with in the chapters above are intimately linked to power relations in society and the disciplining of the social relations that constitute it.

Foucault provides a new way of looking critically at discourses in a different manner from the traditional ideology critique. The concept of ideology has been deployed normally as a critique of false beliefs. Neo-liberalism can thus be seen as an ideology to be "exposed" and the "truth" revealed. This view of discourse rests on a stark dividing line between true and false statements; it is quite unsustainable both in theory and in practice. It also relies on a view of human subjectivity as being either totally deceived by ideology or moving, miraculously, to enlightenment by breaking with it. With Foucault, rather, "we must not imagine a world of discourse divided between accepted discourse and excluded discourse, or between the dominant discourse and the dominated one, but as multiplicity of discursive elements that can come into play in various strategies. . . .

Discourses are not once and for all subservient to power or raised up against it, any more than silences are" (Foucault 1979, 100). Discourses must be seen as unstable and complex, parts of both domination and resistance strategies.

Foucault's theorizing of discourse and domination has great relevance for the development of a transformation strategy for the era of globalization. His great strength, as Howarth notes, is "his refusal to concede to a totalizing and all-encompassing power rooted in the overarching logics of commodification or rationalization, as do other 'critical theories'" (Howarth 2000, 82). From this perspective there is no total system of domination—whether capitalism, patriarchy, or globalization—imposing its logic on people deluded by ideologies of domination. If we were to wait for these delusions to be replaced by a "true consciousness" of the world around us, we might be waiting a long time indeed. We need also to question the assumption in many critical theories that resistance to power and domination is scant and that the "system" has an infinite power to coopt and dissipate it. Rather, we take power to be both diffuse and continuously contested. Resistance is built into the power-knowledge dynamic, as we shall see with the counter-globalization movements that have become a crucial component in the making of globalization as we know it.

So the question of globalization and its contestation can now be reconsidered. It cannot be seen simply as ideology waiting to be exposed by critical analysis. Power and knowledge are bound up in the production of the discourse of globalization. It is a contested discursive terrain where different social groups and political positions vie for discursive hegemony. The irony of the critical position of, for example, parts of the anti-globalization movement is that it grants to globalization an all-encompassing power. From a Foucaultian perspective we can take a more open-ended, less "necessitarian" conception of globalization. We would see how it opens certain political possibilities while closing others. Globalization and the information society it is based on are products of social transformation. There is no simple "truth" that can be set in opposition to this process, such as a new "localism" or "indigenous knowledge," as though these were transparent, self-sufficient, and original. The terrain of globalization is the inescapable place in which a politics of transformation will be forged.

In regard to the definitional issue of globalization, we can agree with Jan Aart Scholte when he argues that "much globe-talk of recent years has revealed nothing new. And yes, loose talking and careless politics has devalued many ideas of 'globalization.' However, these shortcomings do not discredit the concept in every form" (Scholte 2002, 33). Every social and political concept—from democracy to class, from gender to race—is politically and discursively contested. Concepts are sometimes devalued by overuse, and they are often used in less than helpful ways. But the world is changing, and careful usage of the word *globalization* can alert us to the greater "connectivity" of the world today and a greater "spatialization" of social life. The only question is whether it opens up new power-knowledge terrains and confrontations in ways that are conducive to social transformation. I think the evidence is that globalization is indeed a fertile terrain for social transformation.

Social exclusion—the social question of the era of globalization as we have defined it—is equally contested as a discourse. It is a complex notion, its meaning is open, and its politics are variable. We cannot simply react by saying that it has been used by conservatives to coopt and defuse social contestation. Yes, the term *social inclusion* can be given an inflection of integration and even take on racist connotations in relation to immigrants, for example. As with globalization, it is a concept that suffers from conceptual inflation in that it can be used as a polite euphemism for poverty, inequality, and oppression. Nevertheless, even as practiced in the EU, for example, it represents a significant move toward social regulation of the market, especially compared to the dominant Anglo-American model of free-market economics. So, again, we have here a discursive terrain that is complex and needs to be engaged in from a transformationalist perspective, not least when social exclusion is explicitly paired with globalization as the dominant economic logic.

Collective action at global, regional, national, and local levels not only contests globalization and social exclusion but also shapes them as discourses. For the International Federation of Chemical, Energy, Mine and General Workers" Unions (ICEM), the main issue facing workers is that "global corporations need global unions" (ICEM 1999, 42). In taking on that role the unions are not only defending their interests but also shaping the way globalization progresses. Even at its origins, when capital began to "go global" seriously in the 1970s, it was at least in part as a reaction to labor militancy in the advanced industrial societies. Workers now increasingly organize at regional levels, for example in the EU and in NAFTA. They still, even predominantly, organize at the national level and pressurize national governments, but they also engage with local struggles in cities and in rural areas, often in conjunction with other social movements organized around gender or human rights issues, for example.

There are a number of social movements that at different scales, pursue the issue of sovereignty and reflect the still-present history of colonialism. The movement for reparations in respect to slavery had a significant impact at the Durban UN conference against racism of 2001. Indigenous peoples movements in the Americas and Australasia have made significant gains in recent years, at least in part facilitated by the communications revolution associated with globalization. Anti-globalization, anti-colonialism, identity, and sovereignty dynamics merge when indigenous groups take up corporate mining, oil, forestry, or dam projects promoted by imperial powers and their local associates. This cluster of movements is shaping globalization and what we understand by social exclusion as much as (if not more than) the global citizenship and human rights movements promoted within the liberal political parameters of the United Nations discourse. Globalization can, we must conclude, be "civilized" to some extent if not regulated fully by society in the present world order.

The multilayered nature of contestation leads us also to the local manifestations of global processes and social movements. Amory Starr writes of new movements challenging the "commodification" of everyday life: "Including anti-fascist punk youth . . . homeless activists, wealthy historical preservationists, organizers and housing advocates in low-income urban communities, and third world landless workers, these anti-profit movements [all] have important contributions to make to anti-corporatism" (Starr 2000, 64). Indeed, they all contain within them another logic to that of competitiveness, one based on cooperation and sustainability in all senses. Through the World Social Forum (Porto Alegre) these and other social movements across the world seek to articulate an alternative social-development model that is radically opposed to that envisaged by neo-liberal globalization. Yet it many ways this represents an affirmation of a positive or empowered globalization rather than a simple and unilateral denunciation of it as an ideology. This alternative globalization project is well summed up by Castells, who reviews the social movements currently organizing against the new global order and concludes: "It is not a movement against globalization, but a movement for democratic globalization, for a system of governance that would fit democratic ideals in the new context of decision-making that has emerged in a global, network society" (Castells 2003, 154).

The contestation of actually existing globalization by the complex set of social movements now mobilizing at all levels can be seen to address Polanyi's dilemma. How can society regulate the free market? How can the market be "re-embedded" within society? Many of the social movements referred to above are seeking in diverse ways to promote social regulation and the re-embedding of the economy within communities. They are social movements that contest the "commodification" of labor, knowledge, and human beings. Across the world there are diverse movements or processes of economic democratization seeking to re-embed the economy within society. Examples include community economic development projects, the participatory budgets to which we have already referred, and the vast range of practices covered by the term *social economy.* In the Third World an even wider range of social movements is challenging globalization (see Feffer 2002). In different but complementary ways all these countermovements offer an alternative social logic and refuse social exclusion. They complement the movements toward global governance based on reform of UN structures, for example. The main missing ingredient today, as Jan Nederveen Pieterse states, "is a middle ground that intellectually, politically, institutionally, bridges the span between local struggles and global reform, between local alternatives and global constraints" (Nederveen Pieterse 2000, 196). This project would involve the construction of a politics of mediation to match the politics of scale governing both globalization and its contestation.

INCLUSION AND EMPOWERMENT

If globalization generates social exclusion, then a progressive strategy for social transformation, one could assume, will necessarily advocate social inclusion. Yet we have already seen in the section above that contestation of terminology is as important as its more "practical" purposes. The order of things is also an order of words. We struggle for material goods but also over meaning. Thus we must investigate further whether social inclusion is a sufficient as well as a necessary answer to the social exclusion generated by globalization and how an alternative, more radical, strategy of empowerment might be developed. This section is thus a conclusion to this chapter but also to the book as whole. It is here that the transformative approach to globalization and social exclusion must come to fruition, building on the last section, which has already explored the discursive construction of social reality and its contestation.

First of all, we can note with Jock Young that "social inclusion is not simply achieved by being included in the economy, as so many left of centre politicians would seem to believe" (Young 1999, 186). We can, it is quite obvious, be employed and still feel excluded. That is because social exclusion in its social and spatial aspects has a strong cultural and normative aspect. The included space in society is a "good" place, it is "clean," and it is undoubtedly white (see Sibley 1995). In global terms there are the included "homelands" of the West and the excluded marginal spaces of the South and East. This white discourse is one that disempowers. It emphasizes structural forces and minimizes the efficacy of agency. It writes out of this history the voices of the excluded, the oppressed, and the subaltern. While effective as a reformist strategy, in terms of transformation politics it concedes the possibility that the excluded are so due to their own deficits and disqualifications, which bar them from entering the pure, unified space of social inclusion.

The Rockefeller Foundation currently has a major new program entitled Global Inclusion, which, according to the Rockefeller Foundation website, is committed to helping "to broaden the benefits and reduce the negative impacts of globalization on vulnerable communities, families and individuals around the world." While the negative impacts of globalization are recognized, pride of place goes to a broadening of the benefits of this process. The stress is then on those (individuals and communities) who are deemed vulnerable, presumably due to some deficiency in their ability to stand up to the rigors of the market and its ethics of competitiveness. The Rockefeller Foundation advocates an unobjectionable, but ultimately meaningless, inclusive global dialogue to deal (on whose behalf, we might ask) with these problems. The Rockefeller Foundation's objective, in practical terms, is to build knowledge and encourage new practices "aimed at increasing philanthropic investments globally." Just as the early national capitalists dealt with the social effects of capitalism in that era through the Poor Laws, today's global managers advocate philanthropy on a global scale as the means to soften the impact of current capitalist development. Bill Gates of Microsoft is a good example of this tendency, and what is perhaps most remarkable is how far a little redistribution of his vast wealth goes in dealing with basic global issues.

If social inclusion is at best a defensive reformist counter to social exclusion we could, as a first option, take up the universal human rights discourse that has been more prominent at a global level in recent years. Human rights as a universal discourse proclaims (in its French variant) that "every human being, irrespective of race, religion or creed, possesses unalienable and sacred rights." This is vested in "the people" and takes on a distinctively religious air. Juridical equality of all human beings is based on the principle of all "God's children" being created equal. This is a specifically Judeo-Christian perspective and one heavily imbued with Western views of the individual as sovereign and unique. This regime of unalienable individual human rights is legitimated and guaranteed by a structure and discourse of law and rights, which are also presented as universal in validity. For the critics of the Western tradition of human rights such as Alain Supiot we must ask the question: "Are they of universal validity, or is their current cult merely a mask for the worldwide dominion of the West?" (Supiot 2003, 121).

From a global perspective rather than a Western one, it is clear that behind the "universalism" of human rights doctrines lies an ethnocentrism and racism that assumes Western norms and centrality. Other peoples to whom the rules may apply have not created these rules nor do they necessarily subscribe to them. Different cultures are elided by what some critics have described as "human rights imperialism." These "rights" have always been Western, male, and white, whatever gestures are made to multi-culturalism today. In relation to the Third World, human rights are seen as yet another area of deficit with regard to the West, to be rectified along with the penetration of free-market rules and values. While the second option of relativism in regard to human rights may not be an attractive one, we cannot simply take human rights as an unquestioned universal tool for social transformation. In the context of current imperialist conceptions of the Islamic "other," the critique of dominant human rights discourse is understandable, but whether they are or are not truly universal, human rights do still represent some form of protection or legitimate protest against the arbitrary exercise of state power. In the prevailing international political and geo-strategic arena, human rights can be a powerful resource to combat oppression, even if they retain their character as a form of Western fundamentalism that would need to be deconstructed in any global process of progressive transformation.

A third option to take us beyond social exclusion would be the strategy of empowerment that has long had an influence in radical development and adult-education circles. Empowerment is about individuals (and communities) gaining confidence and developing skills that enable them to gain more control over their lives. Caroline Moser defines empowerment as "the capacity of women to increase their own self-reliance and internal strength. This is identified as the right to determine choices in life and to influence the direction of change, through the ability to gain control over material and non-material resources" (Moser 1989, 1815). It should, as a transformative perspective, take us beyond personal development and participation in decision-making to become an active social process. Empowerment cannot be generated from the "outside," as it were; it must come from "within" a community. The concept of empowerment, especially as deployed in community education and gender-awareness training, is akin to Paulo Freire's doctrine of *concientizaçao,* which focuses on individuals development of a critical consciousness the better to transform the world around them.

We can refer to empowering or enabling situations over against disempowering or disabling ones. There is no quick fix in regard to empowerment. Above all, empowerment must be seen as a process and not as a situation of enlightenment to be achieved overnight. Nor does empowerment overcome the divisions within the counter-hegemonic social movements. The landmark anti-globalization protests at Seattle in 1999 were, in retrospect, remarkably white; the World Social Forum events in Porto Alegre have brought together many social movements, but the black and indigenous movements of Latin America are, significantly, absent. So, we must conceive of empowerment in a dynamic and relational way. As Jo Rowlands puts it: "The empowerment of women is a *gender* issue and not simply a women's issue, it is also a class issue, a race issue, and so on, according to the various and changing identities people have. It is about transforming social relations" (Rowlands 1997, 131). The social emancipation process is relational, and it is an ongoing process. It leads us to think positively and practically of the sociology and politics of transformation.

So, finally, we need to consider how we might construct a politics of transformation that would build on the gains of social inclusion, human rights, and empowerment to provide a methodology for global democratization. We have already seen (in Chapters 5 and 6) how a transformative response to gender and race inequalities needs to address the underlying structures in society that produce them. As Peterson sums up: "The historical legacies of masculinism, racism, classism, and colonialism continue to be materialized in stark inequalities. . . . Global regimes continue to favor the interests of rich countries and elites who are advantaged by gender, race, and nationality" (Peterson 2003, 12). To redress this historical and currently reinforced imbalance entails a deconstruction of inequity-generating structures and also of the discursive frameworks that legitimate them. Transformative strategies in the past have been associated with socialism and communism. These, since 1990 at the very latest, are no longer seen as historically viable, but the search is on for radical reformist strategies that would overcome the undoubted social and political risks associated with neo-liberalism. For Brazilian political philosopher Roberto Mangabeira Unger, radical reform is a species of transformative politics that "addresses and changes the basic arrangements of a society: its formative structure of institutions and enacted beliefs" (Mangabeira Unger 1998, 19). How that process can be addressed today, in a multi-scalar way that is cognizant of the complex interlinked nature of today's world, is the key task.

All social structures are socially and discursively constructed and deconstructed. It is through that process of deconstruction that a politics of transformation is constructed. As Sousa Santos declares: "There will be no global justice without global cognitive justice" (Sousa Santos 2003, 2). That is to say, contesting globalization and social exclusion requires building an epistemology more in tune with postcolonial, gender, and race inequalities and perspectives. We need to build the social conditions of possibility for social transformation, not least at the epistemological and educational levels, to develop a way of seeing that is not the dominant one. An emancipatory agenda for learning about the world is outlined (at least in part) in this book, but the task now is to engage with the various movements for social transformation from where we stand in the complex and fluid world in which we live.

CONCLUSION

Globalization, as we argued in Chapter 1, is itself a process of social transformation in that it is changing the whole parameters of economic, social, political, and cultural life in ways that are as yet unclear. The global social exclusion it generates, as described and analyzed from Chapter 2 onward, has deleterious social effects but also tends to create a range of countermovements within society. Some of these merely tinker with the workings of the system or advocate safety nets for those who fall by the wayside. But other reformist measures are more radical and have the possibility of generating transformation, such as, arguably, some of the moves toward global governance. However, the main forms of genuinely transformative social action derive from the range of social movements seeking to counter the hegemony of neo-liberal globalization and to gain social control over the free market. Some of these movements focus on material goods (land, jobs, welfare), others on nonmaterial goods (minority cultural rights, human rights, sovereignty rights). But they are all based on democratic empowerment and point in the direction of social and political transformation of the dominant order.

The period of instability and global conflict following the attacks on the World Trade Towers and the Pentagon, followed by the attacks on Afghanistan and Iraq, has created grave risks for global political stability, not to mention the advancement of global democracy. The gravity of the current crisis should not be doubted. Commenting on the 2003 UN-Habitat study, *Slums of the World,* Mike Davis argues: "The late capitalist triage of humanity, then, has already taken place. . . . *Slums* indeed challenges social theory to grasp the novelty of a true global residuum . . . massively concentrated in a shanty-town world encircling the fortified enclaves of the urban rich" (Davis 2004, 27). The managers of globalization have decided on the order of treatment of those wounded and maimed by the negative impact of globalization, and many millions have simply been condemned to die. This is not just a challenge to social theory but also to the moral and ethical principles raised by today's global polity. The reality is that this polity has taken a negative turn since 2001 with the eclipse of the "pure" neo-liberal pro-globalizers and the emergence of a new breed of "regressive globalizers" who, according to *Global Civil Society 2003* "see the world as a zero-sum game, in which they seek to maximise the benefit of the few, which they represent, at the expense of the welfare of the many, about which they are indifferent at best" (Kaldor, Anheier, and Glasius 2003, 5). Against this gloomy scenario we can posit the continued mobilization of reformist and radical counter-globalization and antiwar movements that are conscious of the risks for global order if the present tendencies toward ever-greater social exclusion continue to prevail.

References

Abbott, Dianne. 2001. Argentina Shows the Reality of Globalisation. Available online.

Albrow, Martin. 1997. *The Global Age: State and Society beyond Modernity.* Cambridge: Polity Press.

Alexander, Titus. 1996. *Unravelling Global Apartheid: An Overview of World Politics.* Cambridge: Polity Press.

Amin, Ash. 1997. Placing Globalization. *Theory, Culture, and Society* 14/2: 123-37.

———. 2002. Spatialities of Globalisation. *Environment and Planning* 34: 385-99.

Andersen, Helen, Ronnie Munck, et al. 1999. *Neighbourhood Images in Liverpool: "It's All Down to the People."* Available online.

Anthias, Floya, and Nira Yuval-Davis. 1993. *Racialized Boundaries: Race, Nation, Gender, Colour and Class and the Anti-racist Struggle.* London: Routledge.

Appadurai, Arjun. 1990. Disjuncture and Difference in the Global Cultural Economy. In *Global Culture*, ed. Mike Featherstone. London: Sage.

Archibugi, Daniel, and David Held, eds. 1996. *Cosmopolitan Democracy: An Agenda for a New World Order.* Revised 2nd edition. Cambridge: Polity Press.

Arrighi, Giovanni, Beverly Silver, and Benjamin Brewer. 2003. Industrial Convergence, Globalization, and the Persistence of the North-South Divide. *Studies in Comparative International Development* 38/1: 3-31.

Aslanbegui, Nahid, Steven Pressman, and Gale Summerfield. 1994. Women and Economic Transformation. In *Women in the Age of Economic Transformation*, ed. Nahid Aslanbegui, Steven Pressman, and Gale Summerfield. London: Routledge.

Babones, Salvatore. 2002. Population and Sample Selection Effects in Measuring International Income Inequality. *Journal of World-Systems Research* 8/1: 8–29.

Bauman, Zygmunt. 1998. *Work, Consumerism, and the New Poor.* Buckingham: Open University Press.

Beck, Ulrich. 2000. *The Brave New World of Work.* Cambridge: Polity Press.

Biemann, Ursula. 2002. Remotely Sensed: A Topography of the Global Sex Trade. *Feminist Review* 70: 75-88.

Birdsall, Nancy. 1999. *Globalization and the Developing Countries: The Inequality Risk.* Washington, DC: ODC. Available online.

Bradley, Harriet. 1996. *Fractured Identities: Changing Patterns of Inequality.* Cambridge: Polity Press.

167

Byrne, David. 1999. *Social Exclusion*. Milton Keynes: Open University Press.

Carnoy, Martin, and Manuel Castells. 2001. *Globalisation, the Knowledge Society, and the Network State*. Global Network 1/1: 1-18.

Castells, Manuel. 1996. *The Information Age: Economy, Society, and Culture*. Volume 1, *The Rise of the Network Society*. Oxford: Blackwell.

———. 1997. *The Information Age: Economy, Society, and Culture*. Volume 2, *The Power of Identity*. Oxford: Blackwell.

———. 1998. *The Information Age: Economy, Society, and Culture*. Volume 3, *End of Millennium*. Oxford: Blackwell.

———. 2001. *The Internet Galaxy: Reflections on the Internet, Business and Society*. Oxford: Oxford University Press.

———. 2003. *The Information Age: Economy, Society, and Culture*. Volume 2, *The Power of Identity*. New edition. Oxford: Blackwell.

Castles, Stephen, and Alistair Davidson. 2000. *Citizenship and Migration, Globalization, and the Politics of Belonging*. London: Macmillan.

Castles, Stephen, and Mark Miller. 1993. *The Age of Migration: International Population Movements in the Modern World*. London: Macmillan.

Cerny, Phil. 2000. Globalization, Governance and Complexity. In *Globalization and Governance*, ed. Aseem Prakash and Jeffrey Hart. London: Routledge.

Chandhoke, Neera. 2002. The Limits of Global Civil Society. In *Global Civil Society 2002*, ed. Marlies Glasius, Mary Kaldor, and Helmut Anheier. Oxford: Oxford University Press.

Chase-Dunn, Christopher. 1998. *Global Formation: Structures of the World-Economy*. Lanham, MD: Rowman and Littlefield.

Chinkin, Christine. 1999. Gender Inequality and International Human Rights Law. In Hurrell and Woods 1999.

Chossudovsky, Michel. 2003. *The Globalization of Poverty and the New World Order*. Canada: Global Outlook.

Chua, Amy. 2003. *World on Fire: How Exporting Free-Market Democracy Breeds Ethnic Hatred and Global Instability*. London: Heineman.

Clarke, John. 2000. A World of Difference? Globalization and the Study of Social Policy. In *Rethinking Social Policy*, ed. G. Lewis, S. Gewirtz, and J. Clarke. London: Sage (Open University).

Clarke, Simon. 1992. Privatisation and the Development of Capitalism in Russia. *New Left Review* 196: 3–27.

Cock, Jacqueline. 1980. *Maids and Madams*. Johannesburg: Ravan Press.

Cohen, Stanley. 1985. *Visions of Social Control: Crime, Punishment and Classification*. Cambridge: Polity Press.

Cohen, Robin, and Paul Kennedy. 2000. *Global Sociology*. London: Palgrave.

Commission on Global Governance, The. 1995. *Our Global Neighbourhood: The Report of the Commission on Global Governance*. Oxford: Oxford University Press.

Cornia, Giovanni, and Julius Kirski. 2001. *Inequality, Growth and Poverty in the Era of Liberalization and Globalization*. Policy Brief No. 4. Geneva: United Nations University. Available online.

Crafts, Nicholas. 2000. *Globalization and Growth in the Twentieth Century*. Working Paper No. 44. Washington, DC: IMF.

Craig, David, and Doug Porter. 2003. Poverty Reduction Strategy Papers: A New Convergence. *World Development* 31/1: 53-69.

Davis, Mike. 2004. Planet of Slums. *New Left Review* 26 (March-April): 5-34. Available online.

Deacon, Bob. 2000. *Globalization and Social Policy: The Threat to Equitable Welfare*. Geneva: UNRISD.

———. 2003. *Global Social Governance Reform*. Globalism and Social Policy Programme Policy Brief No. 1 (January).

Deacon, Bob, Michelle Hulse, and Paul Stubbs. 1997. *Global Social Policy: International Organizations and the Future of Welfare*. London: Sage.

Dirlik, Arif. 1999. Place-based Imagination: Globalism and the Politics of Place. *Review* 22/2: 151-87.

Douglas, Ian. 1999. Globalization *as* Governance: Toward an Archaeology of Contemporary Political Reason. In *Globalization and Governance*, ed. Aseem Prakash and Jeffrey Hart. London: Routledge.

Dunning, John. 2000. The New Geography of Foreign Direct Investment. In *The Political Economy of Globalization*, ed. Ngaire Woods. London: Palgrave.

Eade, John. ed. 1996. *Living the Global City*. London: Routledge.

ECLAC (Economic Commission for Latin America and the Caribbean). 2000. *Equity, Development, and Citizenship*. Mexico City: ECLAC.

Elson, Diane. 1994. Micro, Meso, Macro: Gender and Economic Analysis in the Context of Policy Reforms. In *The Strategic Silence: Gender and Economic Policy*, ed. Isabella Bakker. London: Zed Books.

Elson, Diane, and Ruth Pearson. 1981. The Subordination of Women and the Internationalisation of Production. In *Of Marriage and the Market: Women's Subordination in International Perspectives*, ed. Kate Young, D. Wolkowitz, and R. McCullagh. London: CSE Books.

Enloe, Cynthia. 1990. *Bananas, Beaches and Bases: Making Feminist Sense of International Politics*. Berkeley and Los Angeles: University of California Press.

Evans, Peter. 2000. Counter-hegemonic Globalisation: Transnational Networks as Political Tools for Fighting Marginalization. *Contemporary Sociology* 29 (January): 230-41.

Faria, Vilmar. 1995. Social Exclusion and Latin American Analyses of Poverty and Exclusion. In *Social Exclusion: Rhetoric, Reality, Responses*, ed. Gerry Rodgers, Charles Gore, and José Figueiredo. Geneva: ILO.

Feffer, John, ed. 2002. *Living in Hope: People Challenging Globalization*. London: Zed Books.

Firebaugh, Glenn. 1999. Empirics of World Income Inequality. *American Journal of Sociology* 104/4: 1595–1630.

Foreign Policy. 2002. Globalisation Index 2001. *Foreign Policy* 128: 2-8.

Foucault, Michel. 1977. *Discipline and Punish: The Birth of the Prison*. New York: Pantheon.

———. 1979. *The History of Sexuality*. Volume 1, *Introduction*. London: Penguin.

Fraser, Nancy. 1995. From Redistribution to Recognition? Dilemmas of Justice in a "Post-Socialist" Age. *New Left Review* 212 (July-August): 68-93.

Fukuyama, Francis. 1993. *The End of History and the Last Man*. London: Penguin Books.

———. 1996. *Trust: The Social Virtues and the Creation of Prosperity*. New York: The Free Press.

Garrett, Geoffrey. 2000. Globalization and National Autonomy. In *The Political Economy of Globalization*, ed. Ngaire Woods. London: Palgrave.

George, Vic, and Paul Wilding. 2002. *Globalization and Human Welfare*. London: Palgrave.

Gibson-Graham, J. K. 1996. *The End of Capitalism (As We Knew It): A Feminist Critique of Political Economy*. Oxford: Blackwell.

Gills, Barry, ed. 2000. *Globalization and the Politics of Resistance*. London: Palgrave.

Gore, Charles. 1995. Introduction: Markets, Citizenship and Social Exclusion. In *Social Exclusion: Rhetoric, Reality, Responses*, ed. Gerry Rodgers, Charles Gore, and José Figueiredo. Geneva: ILO.

Goulet, Denis. 2002. *Inequalities in the Light of Globalization*. Joan B. Krok Institute for International Peace Studies Occasional Paper No. 22:OP:2. Notre Dame, IN: University of Notre Dame. Available online.

Gramsci, Antonio. 1971. *Selections from the Prison Notebooks*. London: Lawrence and Wishart.

Gray, John. 2000. Inclusion: A Radical Critique. In *Social Inclusion: Possibilities and Tensions*, ed. Peter Askonas and Angus Stewart. London: Palgrave Macmillan.

Griffin, Keith. 1995. Global Prospects for Development and Human Security. *Canadian Journal of Development Studies* 16/3: 359–70.

Group of Lisbon, The. 1995. *Limits to Competition*. Cambridge, MA: The MIT Press.

Hardt, Michael, and Antonio Negri. 2000. *Empire*. Cambridge, MA: Harvard University Press.

Harvey, David. 1989. *The Condition of Postmodernity*. Oxford: Blackwell.

———. 1996. *Justice, Nature and the Geography of Difference*. Oxford: Blackwell.

Held, David, Anthony McGrew, David Goldblatt, and Jonathan Perraton. 1999. *Global Transformations: Politics, Economics, and Culture*. Cambridge: Polity Press.

Herod, Andy. 2001. Labour Internationalism and the Contradictions of Globalization: or Why the Local Is Sometimes Important in a Global Economy. *Antipode* 33/3: 407-26.

Higgott, Richard. 2002. The Political Economy of Globalisation: Can the Past Inform the Future? CSGR Working Paper. Coventry: University of Warwick.

Hirst, Paul, and Grahame Thompson. 1999. *Globalization in Question*. 2nd ed. Cambridge: Polity Press.

Hobsbawn, Eric. 1994. *The Age of Extremes*. London: Michael Joseph.

Hochschild, Arlie. 2001. Global Care Chains and Emotional Surplus Value. In *On the Edge: Living with Global Capitalism*, ed. Will Hutton and Anthony Giddens. London: Vintage.

Hollingsworth, Rogers. 2004. Taming the Market: Co-ordination of Economic Activities at Multiple Spatial Levels. In *Contesting Public Sector Reforms: Critical Perspectives, International Debates*, ed. P. Dibben, G. Ward, and I. Roper. London: Palgrave.

Horsman, Mathew, and Andrew Marshall. 1995. *After the Nation-State*. London: Harper Collins.

Howarth, David. 2000. *Discourse*. Buckingham: Open University Press.

Hurrell, Andrew, and Ngaire Woods, eds. 1999. *Inequality, Globalization, and World Politics*. Oxford: Oxford University Press.

Hutton, Will. 2002. *The World We're In*. London: Abacus.

Huws, Ursula. 2003.*The Making of a Cybertariat: Virtual Work in a Real World*. London: Merlin Press.

ICEM (International Federation of Chemical, Energy, Mine and General Workers' Unions). 1999. Facing Global Power: Strategies for Global Unionism. ICEM Second World Congress. Durban. November 3–5. Available online.

ILO (International Labour Organisation). 1995. *World Employment Report 1995*. Geneva: ILO.

———. 2004. *The World Commission on the Social Dimension of Globalization*. Geneva: ILO. Available online.

Isin, Engin, and Patricia Wood. 1999. *Citizenship and Identity*. London: Sage.

Jessop, Bob. 2001. On the Spatio-Temporal Logics of Capital's Globalization and Their Manifold Implications for State Power. Lancaster: University of Lancaster, Department of Sociology. Available online.

Jha, Raghbendra. 2000. *Reducing Poverty and Inequality in India: Has Liberalization Helped?* Working Paper No. 204. Geneva: World Institute for Development Economics Research.

Kaldor, Mary. 2003. *Global Civil Society*. Cambridge: Polity Press.

Kaldor, Mary, Helmut Anheier, and Marlies Glasius. 2003. Global Civil Society in an Era of Regressive Globalisation. in *Global Civil Society 2003*, ed. Helmut Anheier, Marlies Glasius, and Mary Kaldor. Oxford: Oxford University Press.

Kaplinski, Ralph. 2000. *Spreading the Gains from Globalisation: What Can Be Learned from Value Chain Analysis?* IDS Working Paper 110. Sussex University:

Kapstein, Ethan B. 2000. Winners and Losers in the Global Economy. *International Organization* 54/2 (Spring): 359-84.

Kastoryano, Riva. 2002. The Reach of Transnationalism. Available online.

Kennedy, Jane, and Michael Lavalette. 2003. Globalisation, Trade Unionism and Solidarity: Further Reflections on the Liverpool Lockout. In *Labour and Globalisation: Results and Prospects*, ed. R. Munck. Liverpool: Liverpool University Press.

Leadbetter, Charles. 2002. *Up the Down Escalator: Why the Global Pessimists Are Wrong*. New York: Viking.

Levitas, Ruth. 1998. *The Inclusive Society? Social Exclusion and New Labour.* London: Palgrave Macmillan.

Lindert, Peter H., and Jeffrey G. Williamson. 2001. Does Globalization Make the World More Unequal? National Bureau of Economic Research (NBER) Working Paper No. w8228. Paper presented at the NBER Globlaization in Historical Perspective Conference, May 3–6, Santa Barbara, California.

Lipietz, Alain, and Eric Saint-Alary. 2000. Social Exclusion in Europe: Meanings, Figures and EU Policies. Available online.

Lister, Ruth. 1997. *Citizenship: Feminist Perspectives.* London: Macmillan.

———. 2000. Strategies for Social Inclusion: Promoting Social Cohesion or Social Justice? In *Social Inclusion: Possibilities and Tensions*, ed. Peter Askonas and Angus Stewart. London: Palgrave Macmillan.

Logan, John, and Harvey Molotch. 1987. *Urban Fortunes: The Political Economy of Place.* Los Angeles and Berkeley: University of California Press.

Madanipour, A., G. Caro, and J. Allen, eds. 1998. *Social Exclusion in European Cities.* London: Jessica Kingsley.

Maddison, Angus. 2001. *The World Economy: A Millenial Perspective.* Paris: Development Centre of the Organisation for Economic Co-operation and Development.

Magdoff, Harry, et al. 2003. What Recovery? *Monthly Review* 54/11 (April). Available online.

Mangabeira Unger, Roberto. 1998. *Democracy Realized: The Progressive Alternative.* London: Verso.

Marcuse, Peter. 1996. Space and Race in the Post-Fordist City: The Outcast Ghetto and Advanced Homelessness in the United States Today. In *Urban Poverty and the Underclass*, ed. Enzo Mingione. Oxford: Blackwell.

Marquand, David. 1991. Civic Republicans and Liberal Individualists: The Case of Britain. *Archive Europeene de Sociologie* 32: 329-44.

Marshall, Gordon, Adam Swift, and Stephen Roberts. 1997. *Against the Odds? Social Class and Social Justice in Industrial Societies.* Oxford: Clarendon Press.

Marshall, T. H. 1950. *Citizenship and Social Class.* Cambridge: Cambridge University Press.

Marston, Sallie. 2000. The Social Construction of Scale. *Progress in Human Geography* 24/2: 219-42.

Marx, Anthony. 1998. *Making Race and Nation: A Comparison of South Africa, the United States, and Brazil.* Cambridge: Cambridge University Press.

Massey, Douglas, and Nancy Denton. 1993. *American Apartheid. Segregation and the Making of the Underclass.* Cambridge, MA: Harvard University Press.

Mazrui, Ali. 1994. Global Apartheid: Structural and Overt. *Alternatives* 19: 185-93.

Mendelsohn, Oliver, and Uppenda Baxi, eds. 1994. *The Rights of Subordinated Peoples.* Delhi: Oxford University Press.

Milanovic, Branko. 2002. True World Income Distribution, 1988 and 1993: First Calculations Based on Household Surveys Alone. *The Economic Journal* 112/51: 92.

Mohanty, Chandra. 1992. Feminist Encounters: Locating the Politics of Experience. In *Destabilizing Theory: Contemporary Feminist Debates*, ed. Michelle Barrett and Anne Phillips. Cambridge: Polity Press.

Molyneux, Maxine. 2002. Gender and the Silences of Social Capital: Lessons from Latin America. *Development and Change* 33/2: 167-88.

Morenoff, Jeffrey D., and Marta Tienda. 1997. Underclass Neighborhoods in Temporal and Ecological Perspective: An Illustration from Chicago. *Annals of the American Academy of Political and Social Science* 551, 59–72.

Morgan, Robin. 1970. *Sisterhood Is Powerful*. New York: Random House.

Morgan, Robin, ed. 1984. *Sisterhood Is Global*. New York: Doubleday/Anchor; reissued New York: The Feminist Press at CUNY, 1996.

Moser, Caroline. 1989. Gender Planning in the Third World: Meeting Practical and Strategic Gender Needs. *World Development* 17/11: 1799-1825.

Munck, Ronaldo. 2001–2002. Argentina or the Political Economy of Collapse. *International Journal of Political Economy* 31/4.

———. 2002. *Globalisation and Labour: The New 'Great Transformation.'* London: Zed Books.

———. 2003. *Reinventing the City? Liverpool in Comparative Perspective*. Liverpool: Liverpool University Press.

———. Forthcoming. *Globalisation and Contestation: Towards a Great Counter-Movement*. London: Routledge.

Murphy, Craig. 2000. Global Governance: Poorly Done and Poorly Understood. *International Affairs* 7/4: 789-803.

Nederveen Pieterse, Jan. 2000. Globalization and Emancipation: From Local Empowerment to Global Reform. In *Globalization and the Politics of Resistance*, ed. Barry Gills. London: Palgrave.

Negri, Antonio. 2003. *Time for Revolution*. London: Continuum.

O'Hearn, Denis. 2001. *The Atlantic Economy: Britain, the US and Ireland*. Manchester: Manchester University Press.

Ohmae, Kenichi. 1990. *The Borderless World*. London: Collins.

———. 1995. *The End of the Nation*. New York: Free Press.

Pasha, Mustapha Kamal. 2002. Predatory Globalization and Democracy in the Islamic World. *The Annals of the American Academy of Political and Social Science* (special issue on globalization and democracy, ed. Ronaldo Munck and Barry Gills) 581 (May): 121-32.

Peterson, V. Spike. 2003. *A Critical Rewriting of Global Political Economy: Integrating reproductive, productive and virtual economies*. London: Routledge.

Pettman, Jan Jindy. 1996. *Worlding Women: A Feminist International Politics*. London: Routledge.

Pierre, Jon, and Guy Peters. 2000. *Governance, Politics, and the State*. London: Palgrave.

Polanyi, Karl. 1957. *The Great Transformation*. Boston: Beacon Press.

Porter, Michael. 1990. *The Competitive Advantage of Nations*. London: Palgrave.

Power, Anne. 2000. Poor Areas and Social Exclusion. In *Social Exclusion and the Future of Cities: CASE [Centre for Analysis of Social Exclusion] Paper 35*, ed. Anne Power and William Julius Wilson. London: CASE.

Prah, Kwesi. 2001. UNRISD Racism and Public Policy Conference, Durban, South Africa. Available online.

Prakash, Aseem, and Jeffrey Hart, eds. 1999. *Globalization and Governance.* London: Routledge.

Putnam, Robert. 1993. *Making Democracy Work: Civic Traditions in Modern Italy.* Princeton, NJ: Princeton University Press.

Rahim, Lily Zubaida. 2001. *Whose Imagined Community? The Nation-State, Ethnicity, and Indigenous Minorities in Southeast Asia.* Geneva: UNRISD.

Rodgers, Gerry. 1995. What Is Special about a Social Exclusion Approach? In *Social Exclusion: Rhetoric, Reality, Responses*, ed. Gerry Rodgers, Charles Gore, and José Figueiredo. Geneva: ILO.

Romero, Mary. 2002. *Maid in the USA: 10th Anniversary Edition.* New York: Routledge.

Rowlands, Jo. 1997. *Questioning Empowerment: Working with Women in Honduras.* Oxford: Oxfam.

Roy, Olivier. 2002. Neo-Fundamentalism. New York: Social Science Research Council. Available online.

Rudolph, Hedwig, Eileen Applebaum, Friederke Maier. 1994. Beyond Socialism: The Uncertain Prospects for East German Women in a United Germany. In *Women in the Age of Economic Transformation,* ed. N. Aslanbegui, S. Pressman, and G. Summerfield. London: Routledge.

Ruggie, John. 1982. International Regimes, Transitions, and Change: Embedded Liberalism on the Postwar Economic Order. *International Organization* 36: 397-415.

Rutherford, Jonathan. 1990. *Identity.* London: Lawrence and Wishart.

Sassen, Saskia. 1999. *Globalization and Its Discontents.* New York: The New Press.

———. 2002. Governance Hotspots: Challenges We Must Confront in the Post-September 11 World. Social Science Research Council. Available online.

Scholte, Jan Aart. 2002. What Is Globalization? The Definitional Issue—Again. CSGR Working Paper No. 109/02. Coventry: University of Warwick.

Sen, Amartya. 1999. *Development as Freedom.* Oxford: Oxford University Press.

———. 2000. *Social Exclusion: Concept, Application, and Scrutiny.* Manila: Asian Development Bank.

Sibley, David. 1995. *Geographies of Exclusion: Society and Difference in the West.* London: Routledge.

Silver, Hilary. 1996. Social Exclusion and Social Solidarity: Three Paradigms. In *Urban Poverty and the Underclass*, ed. Enzo Mingione. Oxford: Blackwell.

Sklair, Leslie. 2001. *The Transnation of Capitalist Class.* Oxford: Blackwell.

Smith, Michael Peter. 2001. *Transnational Urbanism: Locating Globalization.* Oxford: Blackwell.

Sousa Santos, Boaventura. 1995. *Toward a New Common Sense: Science and Politics in the Paradigmatic Transition.* London: Routledge.

———. 2003. The World Social Forum: Toward a Counter-Hegemonic Globalization. Presented at the XXIV International Congress of Latin American Studies Association, Dallas (March 27–29). Available online.

Sparr, Pamela. 1994. What Is Structural Adjustment? In *Mortgaging Women's Lives: Feminist Critiques of Structural Adjustment*, ed. Pamela Sparr. London: Zed Books.

Standing, Guy. 1999. *Global Labour Flexibility: Seeking Distributive Justice.* London: Palgrave Macmillan.

Starr, Amory. 2000. *Naming the Enemy: Anti-Corporate Movements Confront Globalization.* London: Zed Books.

Stavenhagen, Rodolfo. 1999. Structural Racism and Trends in the Global Economy. Geneva: International Council on Human Rights Policy. Available online.

Stiglitz, Joseph. 2002. *Globalization and Its Discontents.* New York: W. W. Norton and Co.

Strange, Susan. 1986. *Casino Capitalism.* Oxford: Blackwell.

Supiot, Alain. 2003. Dogmas and Rights. *New Left Review* 21 (May-June).

Taylor, Ian, and Philip Nel. 2002. "New Africa": Globalisation and the Confines of Elite Reformism: "Getting the Rhetoric Right, Getting the Strategy Wrong." *Third World Quarterly* 23/1: 163-80.

Therborn, Göran. 2000. Dimensions of Globalisation and the Dynamics of (In)Equalities. In *The Ends of Globalization: Bringing Society Back In*, ed. Don Kalb, Marco van der Land, Richard Stanning, Bout van Steenbergen, and Nic Wilterdink. Lanham: Rowman and Littlefield.

Todorov, Tzvetan. 1991. *Nosotros y los otros.* Mexico: Siglo XXI.

Townshend, Peter. 1979. *Poverty in the United Kingdom.* Harmondsworth: Penguin.

Ulshoefer, Petra. 1998. Gender and Social Exclusion. In *Social Exclusion: An ILO Perspective*, ed. José Figueiredo and Arjun de Haan Geneva: ILO.

UNCTAD. 1995. *World Investment Report 1995.* Geneva: UNCTAD.

UNDP (United Nations Development Programme). 1999. *Human Development Report 1999: Globalization with a Human Face.* Geneva: UNDP.

———. 2002. *Human Development Report 2002: Deepening Democracy in a Fragmented World.* New York: Oxford University Press.

UN-Habitat. 2003. *Slums of the World: The Face of Urban Poverty in the New Millenium.* Nairobi, Kenya: United Nations Human Settlements Progamme.

UNRISD. 2000. Globalisation and Social Development after Copenhagen: Pressures, Promises and Policies. Geneva: UNRISD. Available online.

Urry, John. 2003. *Global Complexity.* Cambridge: Polity Press.

Vandemoortele, Jan. 2002. Are We Really Reducing Global Poverty? New York: UNDP. Available online.

Wacquant, Loic. 1994. Red Belt, Black Belt: Racial Division, Class Inequality and the State in the French Urban Periphery and the American Ghetto. In *Urban Poverty and the Underclass*, ed. Enzo Mingione. Oxford: Blackwell.

Wacquant, Loic, and William Julius Wilson. 1989. The Cost of Racial and Class Exclusion in the Inner City. *Annals of the American Academy of Political and Social Science* 501: 8-25.

Wade, Robert. 2001. *Is Globalization Making World Income Distribution More Equal?* London School of Economics Development Studies Institute Working Paper Serices, No. 01-10. Available online.

———. 2004. Is Globalization Reducing Poverty and Inequality? *World Development* 32 (April 4), 567–89.

Walker, A., and C. Walker, eds. 1997. *Britain Divided: The Growth of Social Exclusion in the 1980s and 1990s*. London: Child Poverty Action Group.

Warren, Bill. 1980. *Imperialism: The Pioneer of Capitalism*. London: Verso.

Waterman, Peter. 1998. *Globalisation, Social Movements and the New Internationalism*. London: Mansell.

Weiss, Linda. 1998. Globalisation and the Myth of the Powerless State. *New Left Review* 225: 3-27.

Wilson, William Julius. 2000. The State of American Cities. In *Social Exclusion and the Future of Cities: CASE [Centre for Analysis of Social Exclusion] Paper 35*, ed. A. Power and W. J. Wilson. London: CASE.

Wolfensohn, James. 1997. The Challenge of Social Inclusion. World Bank Annual Meeting Address. Available online.

World Bank. 1986. *Financing Adjustment with Growth in Sub-Saharan Africa*. Washington, DC: World Bank.

———. 1990. *World Bank Annual Report 1990*. Washington, DC: World Bank.

———. 1995. *World Development Report: Workers in an Integrating World*. New York: Oxford University Press.

———. 2000. *World Development Report: Attacking Poverty*. New York: Oxford University Press.

———. 2002. *Globalization, Growth, and Poverty: Building an Inclusive World Economy*. New York: Oxford University Press.

———. 2004. *World Development Report 2004*. Washington, DC: World Bank.

World Commission on the Social Dimension of Globalization. 2003. *A Fair Globalization: Creating Opportunities for All*. Available online.

Yeates, Nicola. 2001. *Globalization and Social Policy*. London: Sage Publications.

Young, Brigitte. 2000. The 'Mistress' and the 'Maid' in the Globalised Economy. In *Socialist Register 200: Working Classes, Global Realities*, ed. L. Panitch and C. Leys, 315–28. London: Merlin Press.

Young, Jock. 1999. *The Exclusive Society*. London: Sage.

About the Author

RONALDO MUNCK is currently working at the President's Office at Dublin City University as strategic director of the university's engagement with globalization and social development. Until recently he was professor of political sociology and director of the Globalisation and Social Exclusion Unit at the University of Liverpool.

Born and educated in Argentina, Munck completed the Ph.D. at the University of Essex. He has published over twenty books in the areas of development studies, labor studies, and the new globalization studies. His recent books include the best-selling *Contemporary Latin America* (Palgrave Macmillan, 2002) and *Globalization and Labour: The New "Great Transformation"* (Zed Books, 2002). Munck is also known for his work on Marxist theory, including *Marx @ 2000: Late Marxist Perspectives* (Zed Books, 2000). He is currently researching the role of global social movements in regulating free-market global capitalism.

Index

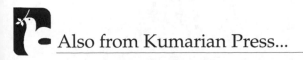
Also from Kumarian Press...

International Development and Civil Society

Creating a Better World: Interpreting Global Civil Society
Edited by Rupert Taylor

Global Civil Society: Dimensions of the Nonprofit Sector, Volume One
Lester M. Salamon, Helmut K. Anheier, Regina List, Stefan Toepler, S. Wojciech Sokolowski and Associates

Global Civil Society: Dimensions of the Nonprofit Sector, Volume Two
Lester M. Salamon, S. Wojciech Sokolowski, and Associates

Going Global: Transforming Relief and Development NGOs
Marc Lindenberg and Coralie Bryant

The Charity of Nations: Humanitarian Action in a Calculating World
Ian Smillie and Larry Minear

When Corporations Rule the World, Second Edition
David C. Korten

Worlds Apart: Civil Society and the Battle for Ethical Globalization
John Clark

International Development, Humanitarianism, Conflict Resolution

Ethics and Global Politics: The Active Learning Sourcebook
Edited by April Morgan, Lucinda Joy Peach, and Colette Mazzucelli

Human Rights and Development
Peter Uvin

Nation-Building Unraveled? Aid, Peace and Justice in Afghanistan
Edited by Antonio Donini, Norah Niland and Karin Wermester

Southern Exposure
International Development and the Global South in the Twenty-First Century
Barbara P. Thomas-Slayter

War and Intervention: Issues for Contemporary Peace Operations
Michael V. Bhatia

Visit Kumarian Press at **www.kpbooks.com** or
call **toll-free 800.289.2664** for a complete catalog.

Kumarian Press, located in Bloomfield, Connecticut, is a forward-looking, scholarly press that promotes active international engagement and an awareness of global connectedness.